the
Pick up
game

the Pick Up game

The proven way to become skilled at approaching and dating women

ROBERT KING

CICO BOOKS

LONDON NEW YORK

Published in 2012 by CICO Books
An imprint of Ryland Peters & Small Ltd
20–21 Jockey's Fields
London WC1R 4BW
519 Broadway, 5th Floor
New York, NY 10012

www.cicobooks.com

10 9 8 7 6 5 4 3 2 1

A CIP catalog record for this book is
available from the Library of Congress
and the British Library.

ISBN: 978-1-908170-97-2

Printed in China

Text © 2012 Robert King
Design and illustration © CICO Books 2012

Illustrator: Karine Faou

 For digital editions visit
www.cicobooks.com/apps.php

CONTENTS

THE PICK-UP ARTIST METHOD

Then he spotted her, the hottest woman in the bar, surrounded by four alpha men. She would have been a seemingly impossible conquest to someone who hadn't been trained in the pick-up arts. Ever since he first started to meditate he had become more centered and happy, freed from a never-ending barrage of useless thoughts and emotions. He was no longer a slave to the overactive mind that had imprisoned him for so long. Seeing the world clearly and truly, he laughed and approached.

His footing was strong and his purpose was clear; nothing out of the ordinary was happening. Like the Red Sea, the men parted without a word. His positive energy immediately drew her in, his first words made her laugh, and his touch was soft but sure. She would be his.

He felt no social pressure; everybody was his friend. To others it probably appeared that she already knew him. To the eye of a quality instructor this was clearly a masterful approach.

He was doing most of the talking, she was holding back, trying not to blow her chance. The other men just watched; they appeared to make some sarcastic comments to each other. They weren't a threat, merely spectators. Despite her beauty his communication was authentic and confident. She had not experienced this kind of approach before and so felt attracted to him. Taking her hand he then led her to the other side of the bar. She shouted something back to the guys, "It's an old friend, don't worry." She was handling the logistics for him.

A PUA method pick-up is undetectable, natural, authentic, and genuine. This book outlines every element required for you to be able to master success with women.

I've dedicated the last seven years of my life to this area, initially for my own development and now to teach it. All of the information found within this book is not theory or statistics. It is the accumulation of many years of infield experience with professional pick-up artists. It has all been tested with success in over thirty different countries.

I took it upon myself to test everything available, talking to women every day for seven years. I think this is most relevant because I was never confident or social, plus I'm now balding. Yet, despite the overwhelming odds, I've dated strippers, models, glamor models, and a famous singer-songwriter, and I've been fortunate enough to meet some amazing women on my journey.

Learning how to become great with women is just like learning any other skill set. It is the same as learning to play tennis, chess, or a musical instrument. It takes time, patience, and, most importantly, requires a good teacher. Having a quality teacher can take years off somebody's natural learning curve. I guarantee that by reading this book you will become much better with women and dating.

Before reading the rest of the book, make sure that you read the PUA Method Terminology section on the opposite page and familiarize yourself with the terms.

PUA METHOD TERMINOLOGY

AFC—*Average frustrated chump*: A man who is currently getting limited success with women.

AMOG—*Alpha Male of Group*: An aggressive male who is competing for the attention of the woman you are interested in.

Approaching: Starting a conversation with a woman or group of people.

DHV—*Demonstration of higher value*: Actively showcasing the qualities you have that women will find attractive.

Direct: Showing interest straightaway when approaching a woman.

DLV—*Demonstration of lower value*: Revealing negative traits to women that they will find unattractive.

IOI—*Indicator of interest*: A signal from a woman that she is interested in you. Examples of this can be her laughing, playing with her hair, or asking you a question.

Indirect: Coming in under the radar when approaching a woman.

Kino: Physically touching someone.

Natural: A man with a lot of alpha-male characteristics. He will have strong core confidence and cool personality traits. He will usually do very well in his social circle but his approaches are often hit and miss. He sometimes manages to say and do the right things, but sometimes he does not.

Opening: Approaching a woman or group of people.

PUA: Pick-up artist.

Routine: A memorized script or game that you use when talking to women.

Routine stack: A number of memorized games, lines, and stories that you can use when in an interaction.

Set: A group of people.

Social proof: Increasing your attractiveness through social alliances; demonstrating that other women are sexually interested in you.

Social robot: A man who has learned a lot of material and taken on the personality of a seduction guru. He does well with women for the first few hours but can't get into relationships and has trouble connecting with people. The robot lives in fear that the person he is talking to will discover his unloved self.

Target: The girl that you are interested in.

Wing: Someone you go out with to meet women.

Zen pick-up artist: A man with strong alpha-male characteristics, who is also very socially calibrated. He has a lot of experience in approaching women and has set sound bites that he uses to generate attraction. He has no problem creating successful relationships; in fact, everybody wants to be around him. He is phenomenally successful at approaching and knows exactly how to give himself the best chance of getting the woman he desires. This man is detached from the outcome and true to himself, but knows how to consistently demonstrate his personality effectively.

MY STORY

Would you believe me if I told you that it is possible to get any woman to feel attracted to you? No? Well, let's take a brief look at my life. Everything that I've written about here actually happened.

WHERE IT ALL BEGAN

I was a chubby nitwit as a child, full of childlike confidence, and always asking questions. Born and raised in a middle-class family in Surrey, England, I lived with my mum, dad, and brother in a medium-size village that had a population of a few thousand people. Mum and Dad didn't have much but through their hard work, often working two jobs at once, they gave my brother and me the best possible head starts in life. We were raised in a nice, smallish village, with plenty of green trees. It was split in two by a road that carried people to work in the neighboring towns. There was just enough to do to stop me from discovering drugs, but very little that I could identify with. There were no landmarks, no soccer stadium, nor anything that was famous in the area. So from a young age I started to form my own identity, which was all about my experiences and nothing to do with cultural influences.

My first school was small and looked like a church. It was situated at the end of my street, about eight houses away. Despite it only being a one-minute walk away, I was usually one of the last to arrive at school in the morning. I'm not sure why I was always late. It could've been because I didn't like it or that I didn't like the feeling of having to go.

MY FIRST CRUSH

I was about seven when I had my first crush. I remember being the first boy in my class to start obviously wanting girls. I wasn't the most alpha male, far from it. I think the wanting was driven more from a desire to be loved.

This crush was on a girl in my class called Nicola. She had blonde hair, blue eyes, and a big toothy smile. We'd often sit next to each other and even held hands once or twice. I remember liking her smell, which was a cross between candy and perfume. This romance

reached its sexual peak one afternoon when she landed a peck on my lips. Sadly, I found out a week later that she had accepted a ring and wedding proposal from a boy named William. I didn't much like this William and so told my friend Jason that I'd caught William urinating in the school hall. A scandal like that for a seven-year-old would probably be like going round your friend's house and doing a dump on his carpet. I really was quite manipulative back then.

I didn't manage to salvage my relationship with Nicola and I heard that she ended up kissing a boy who lived down her street—with tongues and everything. Despite this setback I'd decided that girls were definitely worth pursuing and my arousal mechanism tuned in.

SOLITARY AND SOCIAL

I didn't care for middle or secondary school, and mostly treated them a little like prison. I put my head down and did my time, while trying not to fall in with the wrong crowd. I found school stifling and pointless, and I had the constant feeling of being repressed. I had no idea what I wanted to do with my life, and didn't see how reading Shakespeare would help with that.

I can remember my friends and I being cheeky in class on several occasions. Once during a drama lesson we were discussing ideas for the next school production, sitting around in a circle and talking about the possible characters for a detective play. During this discussion, my friend Tristan shouted out loud that Adam had a hard-on and everyone turned to look. Adam maintains that the bulge was caused by the material that his pants were made of and the angle at which he was sitting. This was a weak plea indeed from someone sitting opposite the only girl in class who had a slight development of cleavage. The damage had been done and the class erupted into laughter. Trying to restore order, the teacher asked what props the detective would need. I cheekily decided to say that a girl in our class called Janet should be the detective's dog. This apparently wasn't the answer that the teacher was looking for, and I was banished to stand and face the wall for the remainder of the lesson. Ironically, showing off and taking things too far is now what I do for a living.

Another dodgy attention-seeking exploit, which I helped co-invent with my friend Robert, was a game called Milk Shakes. It was simple to play. You had to run up behind someone, shout "Milk Shake!" and then shake them up and down. In the beginning this game had innocent intentions, but, just like in the film *Fight Club*, things got out of hand. Our classmates loved it and it was very popular for a whole summer. I think this might have been the time it clicked for me that being fun is a useful attribute to have when with girls. I didn't think of this game as sexual but it does seem a little odd that this is how I chose to express myself socially back then.

Looking back at my school life it might seem like I was social and popular. This wasn't the case, but there were moments of glory in what was an OK but generally uninspired existence. I had mainly male friends and went through periods of feeling social and then seeking solitude. I often sought refuge in the company of animals, my fat cat called Pickles, or the newts in the pond at the front of the house. Sometimes there was stress at home and I believe this is why I spent periods of time in solitude. During my early teens a big, dumb, friendly dog would interest me a lot more than going to a social club. These days I go crazy if I sit in the house for longer than a day. I have to be social. I've discovered that being social is a learned behavior and it is something I help students with regularly.

THE FIRST TIME

I lost my virginity at the age of seventeen, ironically just after I got back from a vacation in Magaluf (or as I was told by my friends when booking it, "Shagaluf"), Majorca. Despite some effort, none of us got laid on that vacation. I did get some kissing action due to my good looks and the girls being very friendly, but I don't think I was in the "I-could-actually-have-sex" headspace. The thought didn't even cross my mind. I was just there for a bit of sun, sea, and sand.

When I returned I met up with my sort-of-girlfriend Kerry. We'd hung out about three times. She had a bit of acne but was definitely a pretty girl, with brown hair and a toned body. I remember her coming round to watch TV and then asking, "What would you like to do?" If my memory serves me correctly, I simply gestured toward my bedroom and that was that.

The sex was bad and I didn't finish. She said that she had had sex before but I guessed it wasn't many times. We were definitely not porn stars and I was understandably nervous. I remember about ten minutes in looking at the clock, trying to work out how much time there was until my favorite TV show *Neighbours* was going to start. It was the episode where Harold got run over. I rolled over, turned on the television, and that was that. She broke up with me a few weeks later.

THE UNIVERSITY YEARS

My next sexual experiences didn't come until I arrived at Southampton University. I studied software engineering but it was never my passion. When it was time to submit our university applications I asked my friend Alan, "What are you doing?" He replied, "Software engineering." I decided to do the same as this would alleviate me of any responsibility of thinking for myself. So, I became a software engineer. Looking back it seems bizarre that I was so whimsical about my future. I just had no idea what I wanted to do. However, the computer skills that I subsequently learned have allowed me to reach you today, so maybe it wasn't a complete waste of time after all and, more importantly, it made me realize that you have to work out what you want in life, particularly when it comes to dating.

My time at university is when I properly buckled down and started practicing the pick-up lines. I remember going out at least every other night in the first year of university, sometimes it was every night. No woman was spared from me and my humorous pick-up lines. Back then there was no dating material available, so I would invent my own techniques when I went out. This dating creativity was all driven by my huge desire to feel loved. A favorite technique of mine and my friend Andy was to get drunk and then take some ice from a glass, approach a woman, and then throw the ice on the floor in front of her. Then in my smoothest voice I'd say, "Now that I've broken the ice, hi, my name is Rob." I believe this classic was stolen from a television show and it amused me greatly.

We also developed another approach. We would go to a quiet pub and order tap waters. We'd look to see which women we liked and then ask the bartender to take the tap waters to them and say it was from the gentlemen at the bar. As the tap waters were delivered, we would pose, trying to look cool. It was funny and actually a good way to open. I recommend it! But we'd rarely be confident enough to start a conversation with the women afterward. Despite my efforts, at my best I was socially awkward and at my worst I was terrible with women.

I remember making some awful dating blunders. For example, I was on a date in a bar with a petite blonde woman and needed to use the restroom. After disposing of the overpriced beer I'd drunk earlier, I went to wash my hands. I personally think it's credit to me for even washing my hands as I'm sure lots of you filthy buggers wouldn't even bother. Anyway, the soap dispenser was wall mounted with a press-down pump mechanism. On pressing down, a shot of white liquid hand soap squirted out at great speed, landing in the center of my shirt. It was not dissimilar looking to the "love" that covered the socks that were lying under my bed at home. Panicking, I applied water to the affected area, which only caused the soap to foam. The more water I added, the larger the area became, and the more foam was produced. I was in that restroom for about fifteen minutes and came out with one half of my shirt soaked. Unsurprisingly the rest of the date didn't go well. She left ten minutes later, saying that something important had come up.

Looking back, it is scary how many times I messed dates up, but I remained undeterred. My success at university was limited. I had a few dates but never any with women I wanted, but at no point did I think, "I'm not cut out for dating." I saw just enough potential to keep persisting with ruthless ambition. What other option was there?

In 2001, whilst in my second year of university, I began avidly reading every self-help and spiritual book that I could get my hands on. I was first introduced to the book *How to Win Friends and Influence People* by Dale Carnegie by my university friend Andy. This popular mainstream book taught me some essential conversation techniques that actually worked and this was the first time I realized that having good social skills was something you could learn. Andy was very similar to me in that he also had a huge needy desire for women to love him.

I found it impossible to focus on my studies. I guess if the love and sex part of your life is not handled, then study just isn't as important. I basically did the minimum to get through university, which is shocking because I'm now, he says modestly, the hardest-working person I know. My two main passions were sports and women. However, I just didn't know what women looked for in a man. I actually thought it was primarily to do with appearance, which confused me a lot because I was a good-looking guy.

I mention that I was good-looking as I believe this was the main reason why I got a minimal level of success with women when I was younger. I looked like a cross between Mulder from *The X-Files* and Tom DeLonge, the guitarist and vocalist of Blink-182. Sadly, my looks (unlike a fine wine) have deteriorated with age.

STUBBORN AS A MULE

Three years after leaving university I had reached the top of the software engineering career ladder and I was getting paid large sums of money. I worked hard and stayed late after work to revise for certifications that I paid for out of my own money. Both my mum and dad were always very hardworking and this was instilled in me from a young age.

I once went for a job interview for the position of a senior oracle database technician. I have no idea what motivated me to go because I had only done one module on databases at university. I turned up for the interview and there were nine other candidates vying for the one position. At that point I could've decided, "I'm probably not going to get this job," and gone home, but I stayed.

We had a two-hour theory exam on oracle databases. After that we went to a hall where some sandwiches were provided and we waited for the next stage. I could've gone after the sandwiches, as I knew that I'd barely answered any of the questions in the exam.

I didn't go home.

I then went to a one-hour psychometric test, which didn't go any better than the theory exam. Despite this, I decided to stick around for the face-to-face interview. Blundering and guessing my way through all the questions, I made it through the interview.

Then I waited for the results of the tests. Here is the moment where I tell you that persistence wins the day! Live the dream! Don't ever give up on life!

I didn't get the job.

What this experience, and others in my life, made me realize, though, is that I'm as stubborn as a mule. Despite overwhelming odds, I'll still foolishly battle on—like Rocky without the theme music. I often wonder what it would be like to have theme music accompanying my life. At least then I'd know when things are about to go right or wrong. Is that a badger in my garden or a serial killer? Maybe I should go out and check. Wait, creepy-horror-movie music doesn't sound very upbeat, I'm outta here!

I did land an IT job about a week later and karma was restored. It wasn't a sexy job but I was happy for a while. However, I soon lost motivation. I felt like I had to push myself through the day. Something was out of alignment.

LEARNING THE ROUTINE

In 2005 I read *The Game* by Neil Strauss, a Rolling Stone journalist who discovered the pick-up artist community and consequently had a lot of personal success. Mystery was one of the lead characters in the book and he became a new role model for me. He seemed like a cool guy and had hot women in his life. The Mystery Method, a pick-up method which he invented, is a logical and scientific approach to meeting women. I managed to get some success with this method, a few dates, and sex. I would repeat memorized lines and routines to women after learning them the night before. It was useful to be given something to say, but most of the time I must have come across as a bit weird.

I have hung out and learned from the best routine-based guys in the world. I met a guy called Max, who at the time taught on Mystery Method boot camps. He was the best routine instructor I had met and was regarded by most as the best in the UK. I had grown a small reputation as being good with women and so we became friends. He took me under his wing and taught me everything. Together we spent many nights in London approaching as many beautiful women as we could.

Max is short, has long hair that he spikes up, and dresses in black clothing. He was fantastic at "opening" (see page 9) and there was no woman that he wouldn't approach. He'd regularly approach women who were out with men already. Many times I've seen women shrug off their boyfriends so they could stay and listen to Max for longer.

One evening we saw a pair of ultra-hot women walking through Piccadilly Circus, London. If you were to rate women on a scale of one to ten, they would both easily have been tens. They walked into a restaurant and so Max and I followed them in. We took a table close to them and we ordered a couple of sodas. Max waited for the waiter to finish taking their order and then took the lead by opening with a scripted routine. Within a few minutes we had both left with their phone numbers.

On another occasion, Max and I were in a coffee shop, but the women he'd approached didn't respond well. Security came over and said, "If you aren't buying anything, then you need to leave." Max just stood there, engaged him in conversation, but refused to move. The social pressure was huge but he knew they couldn't physically touch him.

However, I did begin to notice a few flaws to learning a routine-based system. I got results but, as soon as I ran out of the material that I had learned, I'd lose my confidence and the woman would leave. It was frustrating because I couldn't get past date three, let alone form a relationship, which was primarily what I wanted. I also noticed my general confidence had dropped, which I was surprised by. I had studied the routine method and had approached close to a thousand women by this point and yet I was less confident than ever. I didn't know who I was anymore.

THE NATURAL APPROACH

I decided that this routine-based system of pick-up wasn't the right path for me. It was around this time that I started working on the real me and developing my core confidence. I traveled the world and had amazing times meeting new people and doing new things. I started testing a more natural approach for eighteen months and made significant improvements, but I still wasn't confident. I noticed that even this approach was still reliant on the ego. Rather than learning full scripts, students took on the identities of the instructors. I still hadn't found myself and true consistency at the game was still eluding me.

FINDING MY OWN WAY

Despite making big improvements, internally I hadn't healed. I was still carrying bad childhood experiences and beliefs, and they were preventing me from reaching the next level. I started looking inside myself after reading Buddhist meditation books and from then on I experienced big positive internal shifts. I started reading spiritual material and mainstream self-help books and testing them out. I wasted a lot of time reading poor material and testing things that didn't work, so I had no alternative other than to try to figure things out for myself.

I have lived with monks in Thailand, where they schooled me on their deep-confidence concepts. They taught me the power in letting go, the maybe approach, and going with the flow (see pages 60–64). These are concepts that I teach on boot camp to this day. I have meditated every day for four years and have personally taught over a thousand students the pick-up arts.

I pioneered the Authentic Natural approach to pick-up, which incorporates Buddhist philosophies on a non-religious level. PUA Method is the first company in the world to teach authentic pick-up and meditation at boot camps. PUA Method is the first company to ever teach this live and infield. In fact, I'm one of only a handful of PUA Pick-up Artist CEOs in the world to actually demonstrate, wing, and teach infield. Infield means I'm actually there with

the student talking to women, right by their side to make sure it goes okay. PUA Method takes a holistic approach, which means students gain confidence as well as becoming master pick-up artists. It is the first company to teach meditation and nutrition on boot camps too.

As previously mentioned, PUA Method teaches the most effective parts of natural and routine-based game, but makes sure your confidence grows too. The Surrender (see pages 46–117) covers confidence issues and healing old problems while The Action (see pages 118–188) covers pick-up techniques and gives advice on what to say. I also teach a technical sequence for "opening" (see page 9) that allows anyone to reach over a 90 percent successful opening rate (see pages 74–75). It doesn't matter who you are or what you look like. If you learn the opening technique sequence you will be able to consistently get into conversations with women that you desire.

Over the last five years I've been teaching and demonstrating the authentic, natural approach to meeting women full time with PUA Method. I started out by teaching students for free and then I was forced to charge as demand grew. Teaching is my passion because of the change it's brought to my own life. If I'm not teaching, then I'm reading or practicing and I'm constantly looking for new theories and beliefs that can help other people with their transformations.

I'm at a stage in my life where I have had deep relationships with some truly beautiful women. I have had threesomes, a foursome, and dated strippers and celebrities. On top of that I now have a strong level of confidence and regularly do public speaking and talk with powerful people. I have shaved off my hair, got fatter, and grown a beard all at the same time, but despite this I have learned how to consistently pick up beautiful women.

For the last seven years I have strived for as close to perfection as possible and on most days I would probably put the majority of rock stars' love lives to shame. Most weekends I personally teach on boot camp and I practice approaching every day. What is most important for me is to get otherwise successful men true abundance with women. Scarcity creates anger, which can lead to a downward sequence of fear, grief, and shame. Society might try to convince you that you aren't good enough to date the women you desire. However, I can show that this is not the case; you are good enough for these women, you just need to give your mind evidence that this is true. A world where there is no fear and we all get to live in abundance would be a truly loving, peaceful place.

Now, despite all my success, I don't need any of it. I'd be just as happy sitting in a forest appreciating nature. I always used to think that getting success and love from women would make me happy and fix all my problems. However, it was the journey and not the destination that led me to look inside and become happy in myself.

The best way I can describe it is that being with beautiful women has become normal, nothing more unusual than making dinner. You don't get excited when you make dinner, right? You are just hungry and so you eat, but you can really appreciate and enjoy fantastic food. I now really enjoy having deep connections with women, loving and allowing them to love me without needing it.

Women are just ordinary human beings, but they can also be truly amazing. I don't brag about a woman but I love that feeling of excitement when I'm on my way to meet one. I don't need to get love from anyone, because I share the love of everyone. This duality, taking action without needing the result, is at the core of the PUA Method. It is called "surrendered action," and that is the power that I'm going to give to you.

HOW TO USE THIS BOOK

This book has been organized into two main parts: Part One: The Surrender (see pages 46–117) and Part Two: The Action (see pages 118–188). To become a pick-up artist you need to read and learn both parts. Each time you come back to the book, having got yourself more infield experience, something will jump out at you that you hadn't previously taken on board.

Whatever level you are at, there is something here for everyone. The beginner might focus primarily on what to say, whereas if you're already at a more advanced level, you will probably have a stronger interest in the Surrender sections. But whatever level you are at, to begin with read the whole book without skipping over sections and then use it as a reference for the future.

The person who will get the most from this book will be going out regularly and testing one new thing at a time. He will read a section on qualification and then go out that day and test it on five women. He will learn about meditation and then that day will spend 15 minutes sitting on the floor cross-legged. Even if he doesn't think something is for him, he will test it many times first before discarding it.

THE TWO PARADIGMS OF PICK-UP

There is a misconception that to have strong confidence you need to become someone special, that you must become an important man. This is not the case.

A man who feels important or superior to other men will occasionally have good nights at pick-up, when everything goes his way. However, consistency will always elude him.

The man who is too humble doubts himself too much. He will put others before himself and lack the cutting edge to be able to "close" (see page 9) in a pick-up.

The man who is neither proud nor humble will be able to reach the highest level of consistency with women. He takes on the maybe approach (see page 62) and surrenders to the moment, but still has that inner drive to move the interaction forward.

SURRENDERED ACTION

Typically, the first three to six months of learning pick-up will be spent on studying The Action (see pages 118–188). This is learning what to say, how social interactions work, and how to handle logistics. This learning needs to reach the stage of unconscious competence. This means that you can lead an interaction on autopilot without having to think much about what is happening. If you are already a sociable person, then three to six months could instead become three to six weeks.

As soon as you have reached the stage where you are able to take an interaction through all of the phases and you have sound bites for each section, it is time for you to switch your focus to your inner game, The Surrender (see pages 46–117). It is important to learn how to let go and surrender, especially when under social pressure. Let the world unfold without always trying to figure out what it all means. Don't try hard to make something work, simply allow.

There is a natural flow to life. In the *Tao Te Ching*, a Chinese book of wisdom that has been translated into almost as many languages as the Bible, this natural flow is called the "tao." To fight against this natural flow is a pointless waste of effort. Surrender is one part of the whole and action is another part. You want to join these two together to create surrendered action, without attachment to the result. Dancing is a useful analogy to explain surrendered action—you get into a dancing position, get into the flow of the music, and then let go all at the same time, allowing yourself to move freely with your partner.

Someone who just dances for fun doesn't need to know any steps or dance styles. However, he is probably not going to win any competitions either. A man who is naturally good with women will just express himself and have fun. He will do better than the average man but there is no competition against a professional pick-up artist.

The pick-up artist will have learned the action of how to pick-up. Then he will master the art of letting go, and the surrender. Just like dancing, he will get into position or approach the woman. He will get into the flow of the conversation and the vibe without attempting to force or control it. He will continue to express himself in a way that should move the interaction toward the end goal. He does this freely and without thought because his technique or action is already internalized.

CHAPTER 1: WHAT IS A WOMAN ATTRACTED TO IN A MAN?

The top three alpha-male characteristics that are most attractive to women are:

Confidence—The surrender

Humor—The action

Positivity—The action and the surrender

If you cultivate these three characteristics you will see the biggest change in how attractive you are to women. The first two, confidence and humor, generally take time to achieve and are more long-term aims. If you complete the exercises in this book you will develop all three of these characteristics and more.

WHAT ABOUT LOOKS?

Good looks don't hurt your chances, but they are far from the deciding factor. Was the most popular guy in your school the best looking? Usually, the most popular guy is the confident one or the funny one.

WHAT WOMEN WANT

Men and women are biologically wired to desire different things. Men look at a woman's replication value—how healthy and attractive her children are likely to be—so her hip to breast ratio, facial symmetry, height, hair, lips, and breast and butt size all play a factor. Women look at the man's survival value—how likely he will be able to survive adversity and protect his family—so his confidence, humor, and positivity are the top three characteristics.

A man who is good-looking might get some freebies. For example, some women might approach him or give him signals that they are interested in being approached. Social conditioning teaches women that they should go for a certain type of man, but this type of man isn't what they respond to. A very shallow, un-evolved, socially conditioned woman might primarily focus on a man's looks, but women like this are rare, especially attractive women. A more attractive woman will have gone on dates and generally have better self-esteem than a woman that is typically not as attractive. There are probably many examples that contradict this, but on average it is true.

Women will go on dates with good-looking guys and be very disappointed. The guy is typically shy, acts strange, is immature, and unsure of himself. Some women will understand that looks aren't important for them, while others take a little time to put the pieces of the puzzle together—"So I went on a date with that guy I should be attracted to but wasn't, yet that normal man who made me laugh and made me feel all those emotions, I slept with."

1 PERCENT

Another factor with looks is that if your social skills, confidence, or humor are just 1 percent better than your friend's who is very good-looking, then you will get the woman. I have had many good-looking students (a few male models come on boot camp) and I'm balding, with a regular body. They may look like Brad Pitt in *Fight Club*, yet if I'm just 1 percent better, I end up getting the woman.

What a woman is ultimately looking at is if you feel entitled to be with her. If a man is good-looking, then getting lots of women checking him out in the nightclub will increase his feeling of being entitled. This is a good thing but will lead to the good-looking man fearing the approach and rejection. He has a lot to lose because the woman has put him up on a pedestal and, if he is not cool, she will be disappointed.

TO ILLUSTRATE THE POINT

Colin is a very good-looking guy with strong facial features. He studied software engineering at university with me and is a good friend to this day. Colin generally lacks confidence, is a bit geeky, and can be shy in social situations, although he's much better now than he used to be. In the past I lost count of the number of times women would come up to him in a club, they'd say hi or that they liked him at least once per night. Yet every time he would seem to be able to de-attract the woman. This is a guy who has looks that could grace the cover of a fashion magazine. Yet he only had sex three times over the course of his three years at university, and he is not religious and didn't have a girlfriend.

Now, my housemate Andy was and is a full-on geek. He owns every games console ever created—think Sega Saturn to Dreamcast. He uses phrases such as "It's on like Donkey Kong" and "Locked and loaded." Above his bed he has a massive customized Ms Pac-Man poster. If there was an island of geeks, then he would be The Great Geeker. He isn't great-looking, although he thinks that he is. In fact, he is balding, skinny, and pale-looking.

Now Andy wasn't perfect. He had an ego and a strong need to feel loved. However, this geeky guy, who completely accepted his geekiness, would regularly go out and pick up women. Andy was my main wing back at university and I learned a lot from him.

One of Andy's favorite things to do was to bring a woman back to his room, have sex with her in the dark, and then turn the lights on afterward to reveal his games consoles and posters. He'd then proudly shout, "You've just had sex with a nerd!" I can imagine the poor woman thinking, "Oh my God, what have I done? I had sex with you? You suck!"

Andy didn't have looks but he did have confidence and humor, and he was generally a positive guy.

A man's looks are such a passive thing for a woman that they are basically irrelevant. Make sure you are clean, have shaved, and wear decent clothes and that will be enough for you to date women of unlimited beauty.

WHAT ABOUT MONEY?

Can you name a really fun hobby that you can do every day for free? The only one I can think of is pick-up. Being able to pick-up is the one thing that you can do even if you are poor. The day women start charging us to approach them is the day I'll consider a new hobby. Actually, even if they did start charging I'd probably still do pick-up as it is so much fun. Currently, though, you don't have to pay each woman you approach; this is a free game.

ALPHA AND BETA MALES

Do women find money attractive in a man? There are two types of men: the alpha males and the beta males. The alpha male is the fun, confident guy that the woman will want to sleep with and typically the beta male is the provider who will take care of her.

If you are rich, which category do you think you will automatically be placed in? The beta-male category. Showing the woman that you have money will actually make it harder for you to pick her up. A woman will typically date a beta male for a few months and then at the end he might get sex or he might not. Yet if she meets an alpha male she could end up having sex with him very quickly—possibly even in the club where they met!

I have a friend, Marc, who is a multimillionaire property developer. He is overweight, short, friendly, and fun. He started learning the pick-up artist skill set to improve his dating life. His financial life was taken care of, yet he still couldn't get women in his life. He actually thought that becoming rich would be the way to get women, but to his surprise it didn't help him.

Marc started to become good at pick-up and began to get attraction and dates with women. For over a year his date strategy was to meet the woman at a bar close to his apartment and then go back to his afterward to watch a DVD. This is a good date plan, but he was unable to get "the close." He was sure that the women were attracted to him and wanted to make things sexual, but they changed their minds as soon as they went back to his millionaire apartment.

What was happening was that when the women originally met him they saw him as an alpha male, but when they went back to his really nice apartment and noticed how well he could take care of them, they placed him in the beta male or provider category. They then decided that they weren't going to have sex that night and that they weren't that type of woman. He'd then have to date the woman for several weeks or even months. Occasionally, he'd have sex but mostly nothing would happen but a kiss on the cheek.

As soon as he figured out the pattern he started renting a tiny studio apartment. It is a dark, depressing room, with only enough space for something to sleep on and a chest of drawers. There isn't even a proper bed; it is just a mattress on the floor. Now after a date he takes the woman to his studio apartment and they have sex with the light off. He doesn't get any last-minute resistance or the woman saying that she isn't that type any more. They enter the room and they're immediately all over each other. Now that they have had sex, it will be a lot easier to start a relationship if they both desire it. He can take the woman back to his proper posh apartment and if he wants to build a sexual relationship with her, he can.

Money should be a complete non-factor in meeting and attracting women but it can be a hindrance. If you do happen to be rich, don't panic; there is a solution! The important thing is to let her know that you won't judge her for sleeping with you. The only advantage it may have is giving you access to beautiful women. However, in VIP bars, if you are buying champagne, guess which category you will be placed in when the woman sees this? That's right, the beta-male category. Also, if you do a bit of research it is possible to get into pretty much any VIP club for free if you go on the right night, get a flier, or take women with you.

ALPHA-MALE TRAITS YOU CAN INSTANTLY IMPLEMENT

I mentioned before that the cultivation of confidence and humor is more of a long-term goal and destination. Below I give the four most powerful alpha-male traits that you can implement right now.

1. POSITIVITY

Be positive. Don't talk about how bad your job is, or that you don't like the club, or that your friends are stupid. Be positive about everything, view everything as really cool and fun (see pages 38–39).

2. BE SOCIAL

Talk to everyone in the venue. Don't just approach the hottest women in the bar. Be social with everyone, including the door staff, bar staff, and even guys.

If the woman you are talking to says she has a boyfriend say, "Cool, is he here tonight? Introduce me to him." If the woman is attractive, then chances are her boyfriend is probably a cool guy with other female friends in his life. He could be your new friend or he might introduce you to other women that he is with.

Don't try to seek others' approval—instead offer fun and value to everyone. Women will see this and notice that you are the most popular guy in the venue.

3. DEMONSTRATE STANDARDS AND BOUNDARIES

Show that you aren't a pushover and that you have women in your life already. Don't be happy with the first woman that shows an interest in you. Ask her to tell you something interesting about herself. Qualify her (see pages 155–157).

Make sure that you don't accept poor behavior. If you think she's expecting you to buy her a drink say, "You get the first round and I'll get the second round." If there is some attraction, there is a good chance she'll say yes to this. Or even better say, "If you kiss me, then maybe I'll buy you a drink."

4. LOWER YOUR STANDARD FOR HAPPINESS

"If I am opening, then I am happy."

Remember this phrase and repeat it to yourself when you are out. This is my own personal standard of happiness when I am out. If I'm not "opening" (see page 9), then I shouldn't be happy because I'm not taking action. If I'm approaching, then regardless of the outcome I can be happy because I am growing.

With this standard for happiness you give yourself the best chance of having a successful time.

OTHER ALPHA-MALE CHARACTERISTICS

Although I have covered the top three alpha-male characteristics, there are others which are important to your success as well.

PRE-SELECTION

A man's attraction for a woman is like a light switch: it's either "on," you would have sex with this woman; or it's "off," you wouldn't. Men are a lot less picky personality-wise than women about who they sleep with. But when seeing if the woman is suitable for a relationship, other factors come into play.

A woman's attraction for a man is like a volume knob. It takes her time to make a decision about you. She is looking at your alpha traits and seeing whether the man you are showing is actually who you are and not fake. Unless you are peacocked /dressed in a cool way, standing out, or have obvious value, the woman will be indifferent to your interaction at the beginning. This is not because she doesn't like you; she just doesn't know you yet.

Pre-selection happens in both humans and animals. It is when you demonstrate that other females are sexually interested in you. This will drastically speed up the seduction process. The woman won't need to check your behavior because another woman has already done that for her. If you have female friends or are very good-looking, then your girlfriend will be able to constantly see that you are a desirable man. If you don't have these advantages, then you can manufacture environments where you are desired. Environments where you are the leader or where there are a lot more women than men are always favorable.

When I walk into a bar with two of my male friends I am a lot less attractive to another woman than if I was with two female friends. Having female friends and going out with women rather than men well help you immensely in meeting and attracting a new mate.

If you don't have women with you, then it can help to mention that you have women in your life, but it is always more powerful to actually demonstrate you are desired than to just tell her. The number one priority must be to get female friends and invite them out. Don't sleep with them, just hang out and have fun.

Kiss marks on your cheek or shirt are great. Other women will see the kiss marks and realize that you are a desired man. Get your mum to give you a kiss before you leave the house if you have to. Women kissing your bald head is also a major positive, so don't wipe those marks off.

When talking to a woman, be aware of who is exerting the most effort. If she is sitting and you are standing, then it's best to find a chair or get her to stand. If she is leaning back against the wall and you are leaning into her, then it's best to reverse that situation. Leaning back against a wall and letting the woman lean into you will result in increased attraction from every other woman who sees this. It looks like the woman is trying to pick you up and so you become pre-selected.

Many women will still be interested in you even if they see you kissing other women. One particular night at a club about two years ago resulted in what I call a "feeding frenzy." My wingman and PUA Method instructor Cupid and I set ourselves a friendly challenge. The first one of us to get a kiss was the winner. I turned round and saw a woman I'd seen waiting at the bus stop. I walked up to her, teased her, and kissed her within about three minutes. It was very funny as the game was over almost before it began. This then kick-started a great night and we started kissing women all over the club. I walked up to two women and kissed them both within minutes. Cupid got four kisses and I got six in one evening, all different women, no sharing. We became the rock stars of the nightclub. I kissed one woman and a woman that I had previously kissed saw this and immediately started making out with the nearest man she could find. Emotions were high and pre-selection is a very powerful tool to use. Let women see that other women want you. Everyone wants someone popular.

MEN FOLLOW YOUR LEAD

When we were all cavemen there would be one alpha male who had all the women and food, plus a couple of beta males who got some scraps. Women always want the man who can provide the best survival chances for their offspring, so leading other men will improve your survival value a lot. When you lead the men, the women follow.

Typically, alpha males are friends with a few alpha or beta males that they can trust. You will often notice confident guys set a frame of either "impress me" or "you can't enter into my social circle." These guys have recognized that when they dominate other men, women respond better.

If you want to enter a social circle but don't want to impress the alpha male, then be aware of the value that you are offering. The alpha male might value the following:

- **Can you improve his humor or make him laugh?**

- **Can you improve his financial situation?**

- **Can you improve his health?**

- **Can you improve his social status?**

- **Can you improve his survival value by being able to protect him in a conflict situation?**

- **Can you improve his replication value by introducing him to women?**

By being aware of the value that you offer to other men you can become a man all men want to have around. A man's man.

There are similarities to the animal kingdom. A rogue or traveling monkey that wants to join a troop will observe it first. He will notice which monkey is the alpha male and then decide whether to befriend the alpha male and then figure out a way to defeat him later on or attack him straightaway. The alpha male has access to the females and the food. It is useful to remember this when you are out with girls.

Russell Brand wears eye make-up, wears women's clothes, has a strange hairstyle, and is super-skinny. He is a really easy target for abuse from other men, yet no one bothers him. Why is this? It is because he has practiced social sparring with friends, on the comedy circuit, and on television and radio for years. He's proved himself several times. Now it is well known by comedians that he can reduce even the most confident alpha males to beta wrecks. An example of this was on the TV show, the *Big Fat Quiz of the Year*. He was asked, "Why do you dress so bad?" He replied, "At least I've made an effort, whereas you look like you've been mugged by C&A in an alley. Now be about your business." This was all done in a cheeky, fun tone, the rival comedian was destroyed, test passed.

Generally, be friendly to other guys. This means building commonalities and sharing experiences. Dancing, drinking, or playing pool together are all good. Friendships are built on having things in common and sharing a similar view of the world.

If you're out with a woman who isn't your girlfriend yet, then it is usually better to ignore a man trying to enter your conversation and continue talking to the woman. This is not done in a mean way, it just communicates that the guy is such low value that you don't even realize he is there. A lot of the time I don't even notice these guys. This then lowers their value and they will either leave or supplicate to you. This actively demonstrates in front of the woman that men follow your lead or want your approval.

With friends, treat them as equals but have strong boundaries of what behavior you do and don't accept. If your friend gets cocky, then respond with something better, ignore it, or say "respect." Saying something funnier will cause the friend to "beta," ignoring the behavior lowers his value, and saying "respect" sets the frame for the woman that he was trying to impress you.

Don't put yourself in a situation of taking a woman that you like to an environment where there will be alpha guys. Take a female friend instead to get experience of how to deal with this situation, but don't risk it with a woman who you really like.

HUMOR

Laughter has been around since the dawn of time. Even monkeys bond and communicate with one another through laughing. It shows they are having fun and are not being serious, which is especially important during play fights.

Most women say that a sense of humor is a very important characteristic in a man, and they are right. It shows social intuition, the ability to provoke positive emotions in others, and it creates closer bonds between people when they share a laugh.

The ability to be humorous can be learned, as can being confident, sociable, or fun. The important part of developing a new skill is to plow through the early awkward phase until it becomes more natural.

One of the basics of being humorous is to make sure that you are trying to amuse yourself. Things that I personally find funny are often things that shock other people. I find it entertaining to see how people react to certain things (usually sexual) and just cause drama and amusement for fun.

Humor comes from a place of commonality, love, and surprise. When you're in the right mindset, anything can be funny. Watch your favorite comedians and repeat some of their jokes when you are out. You will start to notice a pattern in comedy, which is the setup and then a surprise. This may well lead to moments when you accidentally say something funny. Gradually your humor muscle will increase.

The key element of humor is to lead a story in one direction and then deliver a surprise punchline in another direction that the listener wasn't expecting. For example, "This is my friend Jack, he is an awesome guy—fun, friendly, caring. Shame he's a virgin." The setup and the surprise, it is very simple. The conversation has set a tone of me giving props to my friend and then I embarrass him. A bit mean but funny.

Comedians can be very funny and not get laid. Often times that is because their humor crossed over the boundary into "clown mode." Clown mode is when you are trying to get a reaction and not just having fun for yourself. Examples of this could be jumping around, telling too many jokes, looking for the woman's approval, or exhibiting low-value behavior for a laugh. If you are having fun, chances are you will be given a pass, even if the joke isn't that good, so don't cross over into clown mode.

Try to live your life in a way that is good and giving. If I was to behave like a right idiot, how could I expect people to love me and laugh at me when I'm out socializing? Try not to lie, cheat, steal, bitch, and all those other things that we got told not to do at school. Try to be nice and look for the best in all people. This frame helps remove passive anger, which can stop an otherwise awesome joke being funny just because you sounded a little bitter.

POSITIVITY

Being positive is definitely one of the most attractive qualities a person can have. It is something that cool people instinctively understand and un-cool people don't. It is part of the secret language of communication that I was never aware of, until I studied it.

Being a positive, happy person shows the woman that you are able to take care of yourself. A man who is emotionally flimsy will leave the woman feeling unsure and unprotected. She will be forced to take on the role of being the man and so become less feminine.

A strong, masculine character will be in control of his own emotions. His emotions won't change much due to external circumstances. He is resourceful enough to make sure he is happy and, if he's not, then he will take action and do something about it. He doesn't moan or complain about his lot.

The feminine character is a lot more in touch with emotions and will thrive on them to feel alive. For a woman to enjoy her emotions she must feel sure that the man will stay strong and be able to protect her. A positive masculine man won't react to her emotions, which would lead to more drama. Instead he will stay rooted to his masculine presence, keeping cool and calm. Soon enough her emotions will pass and she will respect you for being strong and together.

Being positive is not about ignoring awkward situations or difficult events. Instead, rather than dwelling on the negative, you decide on what is the best action to take and then follow through.

When you feel happy and positive inside it will project outward, turning you into a people magnet. People love to be around others who make them feel good. This principle applies to making friends as well. Two of the main driving forces of human nature are to avoid pain and move toward pleasure. A positive, happy person will automatically make other people around them feel good by their presence alone. Famous examples of this that spring to mind are Lewis Hamilton and David Beckham. Their energy alone is appealing.

This is why a positive man is very attractive to happy women with high self-esteem. They subconsciously realize that the man is likely to be more ambitious and fun. Negative people tend to gravitate toward other negative people. You will attract women who are like you. If you go to the gym a lot, then you will start to attract athletic women into your life. If you are negative and depressed, you will attract a similar type of woman.

Being positive is a screen I use when meeting new people. If I meet a negative woman, I will not start being negative and down so I can connect better with her. Instead, I'll stay positive and continue to have fun. If the woman remains negative, then I'll usually find someone else to talk to. I recommend that you treat your mind like a gate and only let things that help enter. Limiting beliefs and negative mindsets won't help and should be avoided as much as possible.

Love your family and your friends but also surround yourself with positive people. Who you spend time with will have a direct influence on you as a person. Be selective about your friends and the environments you spend time in.

Changing your mindset to a positive one will change your physiology, too. When you are feeling great, how do you usually carry yourself? When I feel amazing my back is straight, my voice is loud and clear, I smile, my breathing is deep, my eye contact is strong, and I move with purpose. When I have negative thoughts and am feeling down, what happens to my body language? Yes, you guessed it. My shoulders slump, my eye contact is weak, my voice is quiet, and my breathing is shallow. Which guy do you think a woman is going to feel more attraction toward? When approaching women don't beat yourself up for being in a bad mood. Just accept that whatever negative state you might be in at that moment will pass and do what you were going to do anyway. Be positive about approaching, you never know what can happen.

When you are positive, everything you dream of seems possible and it probably is. The actor, Will Smith, once spoke in an interview about never giving up: "The guy that keeps trying and stays positive, he's the one who's going to get that lucky ball, or the one that gets that great opportunity. He's putting himself in a position to receive it."

Being positive is a state of mind. If you have sat indoors all day on your own, it might be harder for you to be positive. Make sure your life has balance and that you aren't missing anything. Negativity usually comes from a place of frustration and the feeling of not being in control. If you are generally a positive person but have been feeling negative recently, then be proactive, find out what's causing it, and make a change. Whenever you enter a negative state, do something to snap yourself out of it. Dance, go for a run, or sing out loud—these are all good things to do. This will condition you to be in a positive state more often.

Finally, the state of mind you are most used to accessing will become your default state. For instance, if you are mainly negative, then you can have a positive moment but soon after you will go back to finding something wrong with the world. To train yourself to become more positive you must snap out of any negative feelings. Become aware of them and understand when they happen. These are called triggers. When you know what triggers your negative emotions you can gain control over your happiness. Continue to surround yourself with positive people, books, and other influences.

A MAN WHO TAKES ACTION

An alpha male will have a mindset of "I can do that." He will then follow through and do it. It is not arrogant to think that you can do something. It is arrogant to talk about doing something, then rest on your laurels and not actually do it. Taking action by doing things that will take you closer to your goals and improve confidence is one of the key ways to build self-esteem.

Taking action also comes down to whether you are a man who does what he says. For instance, if you start a new fitness regime and then don't turn up to the gym, how will you follow through in the future when you set yourself another goal? Many people make big statements like "This year will be my year," and then one month later they are back stuck in the same rut. Make sure you are a person that not only says he is going to do something but follows it through as well. A winner.

It is important not to over-plan when looking to take action. Planning a little is fine, but the main thing is just to do something. Taking action, however small it might be, will give you momentum. For example, for a person who is overweight it will not be important to find a great trainer or a workout plan. Instead they just need to find someone that goes to the gym or takes a walk around the block regularly and will drag them out of the house on a cold winter's day.

AMBITION

Ambition is a very attractive quality and something that all women look for in men. An attractive woman usually won't even mind what your starting situation is. You can work in a fast-food restaurant as long as you have goals and you are making progress toward them. When on a date with a woman, tell her about your dreams and goals and watch her eyes glaze over with desire. An ambitious man is a more exciting prospect than a man who settles.

There is often a lot of confusion over whether it's OK to have goals and dreams and yet still remain in the now and Zen. Personally, I think balance is key, as with anything in life. Set goals for the future and then return to a present state of acceptance to carry them out. Your mind is there to be used. It is just that the majority of time-wasting thoughts pollute it and create stress.

If you aren't improving, then you are stagnating. Having goals that you meet will build self-esteem. Ambition can be for anything as long as you have something you are working toward and aren't being lazy. I personally think it's very difficult to be positive and happy if you aren't growing as a person. If I don't do anything productive during the day, then I usually end up feeling down and depressed.

From my experience, women are like talent scouts and are looking for the next big thing. Having dreams that you are moving toward will make you a very exciting prospect indeed.

THE SPIRITUAL GODDESS PICK-UP

The following is a true account of an approach I made some years ago. I've included it because it perfectly demonstrates how to take action, whilst at the same time being authentic and true to yourself.

I was walking down the street, minding my own business. Then I saw her, skipping down the road in front of me. She was wearing a long black pleated dress, white trainers, and a tight flowery top. As she turned round to check the traffic behind her, I could see that she had a model yet "girl-next-door" face. She was slightly taller than average, but what struck me was that she had really good energy and a freeness that is so rare to see. She would walk for a few paces and then run for a little bit, her long blonde hair flowing behind her. She seemed so at peace and full of love. Attractive, free-spiritedness, good energy... There was no choice: I had to approach!

Before I had time to think about what I was doing my legs had started moving. As I started to run towards her my only thought was, "what's my opener?"

"Hey, I love your style. I had to come over and meet you."

She stopped and smiled.

From years of practice, I knew that my approach was perfect. I'd left enough space, approached her at the correct angle, stopped her and then crossed her path. It was as if I was on autopilot. Keep talking...

"You remind me of my time in scouts; I could imagine you singing me a song round a campfire. I love your hippy look."

She started to giggle

The way I opened was completely authentic; my words, thoughts, and actions were all in alignment. I could tell that she felt relaxed and trusted me. I had no hesitation and didn't give a passing thought to what passers-by were thinking. My intent and purpose were clear: I was going for what I wanted. There was no confusion.

I checked to see if I needed to time constraint—no, she looked happy to talk. I looked to see if I needed to set the frame. I would normally do this by telling her how random it would be for me to just run up to someone but that she was so gorgeous that I had to come over and see if had more going on that just her good looks. Again, she looked happy with situation. She was a free spirit.

I desperately wanted to find out everything about her. I was aware how rare it was to meet a woman so free, and not be consumed by fear or worry about what other people around would think. However, I decided to play a solid game and not rush things. The courtship dance began—two steps forward, one step back.

Conversation took the form of a statement followed by a question. I moved her to the side of the pavement away from the barrage of shoppers. As the conversation continued, I gave 90 percent of myself to her and just held back on the other 10 percent. I gave her an occasional light tease:

"Oh my God, if we were to hang out you wouldn't hug trees and make daisy chains in front of my friends would you?"

She liked me. Her legs were crossed, she was playing with her hair. She starting asking me questions now, such as, "where are you from?". I began to qualify her. I found things out about her that interested me.

"Are you vegan?"

"Are you positive?"

"Do you do any sport?"

"Do you ever do yoga or meditation?"

She ticked a lot of the boxes. I felt even more interested in her but I also knew that at any moment she could do or say something that could disappoint me. So far she was doing well, and I told her so.

Her body was not as curvy as I would usually like but her model face and amazing spirit made up for this. What was she up to today? Not much, as it turned out, just shopping and meeting a friend later in the park. My 10,000 plus approach experience told me that she would come on an instant date with me now. Unfortunately I had to be somewhere and was in a rush and—sometimes—work has to come before fun.

I number closed and said that if she was in an adventurous mood, maybe we could go for cocktails later. She smiled and said "maybe." Cheeky girl, she was now holding herself back. I liked this though, it showed she had standards and I always love a challenge.

Later that night we did meet up for cocktails. The night ended in a crescendo of spiritual orgasms.

This pick up is pretty standard for me and how a lot of my daytime approaches will go. My advice as always, is to be authentic, go for what you want and play the pick-up game.

The Surrender

(Yin)

Chapter 2: Zen

WHAT IS ZEN?

The word "Zen" in Japanese means "to meditate." That being said, there is a lot more loveliness to Zen than just meditation. Zen is a part of Buddhism and focuses on mind and body training, with its aim of awakening (enlightening) the individual.

Buddhism uses the teachings of the Buddha, who is believed to have lived and died within the period 600–400 BC in India. His teachings focus on combatting the three evils of society:

- Violence—This must be avoided in all forms against all things.
- The self—The holding on to a false sense of self should be stopped. The self is an image in your mind of who you are. This leads to much suffering and a lack of contentment and happiness.
- Death—The Buddha believed that death was not the end of life, and that its outcome can be changed by reaching enlightenment (freedom from the mind).

Becoming Zen means you remove your fake self and discover your real self. This leads to self-esteem, confidence, positivity, centeredness, happiness, and all those other characteristics that women can't help but be attracted to.

WHAT IS ZAZEN?

Zazen is at the heart of Zen Buddhist practice and basically means "seated meditation." It represents the doorway to enlightenment, the pathway to glory. Zazen practiced properly is the concentrated effort of emptying the mind.

> *All thoughts whether positive or negative, are mutable and imperma-nent, they will always have a beginning, middle and an end. It has been commonly noted that thought is the sickness of the human mind and from a Buddhist point of view, that is very accurate.*
>
> **The Three Pillars of Zen by Philip Kapleau**

Have you ever had something on your mind and then started to feel unwell? This is because your energy is becoming toxic.

Unfortunately, the majority of human beings will live anxious, restless, and half-crazed lives. Their minds, filled with delusion, are turned upside down and back to front. The only solution available is that we return to our original perfection. As infants we had no false image of ourselves, we just were. The following text describes enlightenment, or Kensho.

The mind of a Buddha is like water that is calm, deep, and crystal clear, upon which the moon of truth reflects perfectly. The normal mind is like murky water, constantly being churned by gales of delusive thought. It is no longer able to reflect the moon of truth.

As long as the gales of delusive thoughts are churning the water it will be impossible to be able to ascertain true nature and the untrue. Therefore these winds must be calmed through the act of practicing Zazen. The churning will stop, the water will clear. Then you will realize that the moon of truth never stopped shining because now you can see the reflection.

The Three Pillars of Zen by Philip Kapleau

THE BENEFITS OF ZAZEN MEDITATION

In this book I talk about using Zen as a way of benefiting mind and body, rather than as a religious persuasion. Meditation might sound a little "out there" but let me expain how practicing daily Zazen meditation will benefit your game:

1. It will allow you to get in touch with yourself beyond your physical presence and mind. It will guide you toward the deep true you, the spiritual you, a true realization of "who am I?" on a deep level that only really comes in the form of spiritual enlightenment. This will remove ego and the need for approval, which 99 percent of guys have when approaching a woman. The "Do you like me?", "Can you validate me?" are sub-communicated. When you meditate, you feel who you are and you will not need anyone's approval.

2. Practicing Zazen twice a day, 15 minutes a session, for a month, will give you a much deeper sense of who you are. A man who is in touch with his core is very attractive. This is masculine energy, centered and unreactive.

3. It will help stop the endless thought loops that go on in the mind. This will lead to more control of your own state. The average person is bombarded by lots of mental images, being played over and over again. This is both energy-sapping and tiring, leading to mood swings. Zazen will quieten your mind and condition you to become more aware of your thoughts.

4. A lot of the thought loops that the mind plays are using up unnecessary energy. This is often why stressing about something will quickly lead to tiredness, or sometimes sickness. Instead of overanalyzing, simply look at the options and take the right action based on your decision.

5. "See reality clearly rather than a false perception of reality created by your mind. Imagine true reality is like water. When you have an over-active mind, it is clouding it into a thick sludgy Amazon river." This quote is from *Zen Mind, Beginner's Mind* by Shunryu Suzuki. When the mind is active, nothing is clear because of your thought loops, rationalizations, and beliefs. For example, a feeling that your girlfriend is cheating on you is usually self-manufactured.

6. Zazen develops the power of concentration, allowing you to focus on whatever you want to achieve. Most of the time people try to do lots of things and get easily distracted. With a concentrated mind you become a lot more focused and efficient, resulting in more free time. So when you are approaching women, instead of reacting to bad comments or strange facial expressions, you stay focused.

7. If you worry about approaching women, then you are probably playing negative thought loops in your mind. These thought loops happen in milliseconds and will change your mood instantly—happy one second, depressed, angry, or frustrated the next. Zazen quietens this barrage of unwanted mind noise, so when approaching a woman you will be completely refreshed and in the present moment. Negative emotions lead to negative energy, weak smiles, dull eyes, and nervous mannerisms. When you remove these negative thoughts, you will stay positive and happy.

8. Meditating for long periods of time will allow you to realize that it is possible to be completely happy just being with yourself. When sitting in a meditation position for a couple of hours, you realize on a deep level that you need nothing external to be happy. When you approach women with this realization, you will be non-needy and unreactive, even to the most beautiful of women. Conversations with women possessing such beauty that you know her babies would contain perfect DNA will not even phase you. You realize that chasing beauty is a game, but you don't need it because you are happy with whatever happens.

THE FIVE TYPES OF ZEN

1. BOMPU (ORDINARY ZEN)

Bompu is free from any religious content and is for anybody and everybody. It is Zen that is practiced purely in the belief that it can improve both physical and mental health. It rarely occurs to most people to try to control their minds; this basic training is absent from most educational upbringings in the Western world. Bompu Zen and Loving Kindness Meditation (see pages 57-58) are currently taught on PUA Method boot camps. They both tie in with dating and self-development.

2. GEDO (AN OUTSIDE WAY)

This Zen is taught from a religious point of view but is not part of Buddhism. A lot of yoga, quiet sitting, and contemplation practices in Christianity come from Gedo Zen. Gedo Zen is also used to cultivate various supernormal powers or skills outside of an average person's reach. There have been cases of practitioners of Gedo Zen being able to make other people move without moving a muscle themselves, walking over sword blades, and staring at birds until they become paralyzed.

3. SHOJO (SMALL VEHICLE)

This "small vehicle" is used to take yourself from a place of delusion to enlightenment. Shojo Zen focuses on achieving peace of mind, but segregates you from the rest of the world that is labeled evil and bad.

4. DAIJO (GREAT VEHICLE)

This is true Buddhist Zen and its main purpose is for you to seek and realize your essential nature from within your daily life. The Buddha taught this form of Zen for 50 years after realizing his own self-nature.

5. SAIJOJO (HIGHEST VEHICLE):

This is the peak of Buddhist Zen and was practiced by all Buddhas of the past. It complements Daijo Zen and, when practiced correctly, it encourages you to sit in contemplation with full faith that you will reach the day of enlightenment.

HOW TO DO ZAZEN

If you suffer from a bad back or any other health problems, it's a good idea to consult your doctor before starting any meditation. You need to practice Zazen somewhere that doesn't have lots of distractions. If possible, select a room that is quiet. Sit on a cushion placed on the floor; your bed is associated with rest and other activities, so it is not an ideal place to practice on. The key is that you need to be somewhere quiet—that is not visually stimulating—where you can keep your mind taut and back straight.

I recommend that if you practice Zazen in the evening that you turn the light off and light some candles. When the light is on I find it difficult to distance myself from my gruelling work day and to get in touch with my spiritual core. Candles will become a ritual and you will quickly associate that it is now time to meditate.

SITTING POSITION

If you have not been taught how to sit in the half-lotus or full-lotus position then I recommend that you just sit cross-legged. It is possible to cause an injury when sitting in an uncomfortable position for extended periods of time. The positions are shown here but you could consider going to your local Buddhist center and ask to be shown.

HALF-LOTUS POSITION

FULL-LOTUS POSITION

EYES

With a straight neck and your head pointing down slightly, have your eyes focused on the ground about 3¼ft (1m) away from you. Be careful not to let your head slump or fall—if this happens become aware of it and return to the normal position.

POSTURE

Fold your hands in your lap, with one hand placed on top of the other. Make sure that your spine is erect and straight at all times. Try not to make it so straight that you feel superior but also not so slumped that you feel lazy or not worthy; both of these feelings are attached to a false sense of self, which is also known as the ego. When the body slumps, undue pressure is placed on the internal organs, which will interfere with concentration.

FOCUS

Zazen focuses on calming the mind. Fleeting thoughts entering your mind while exercising Zazen are not a disaster. In fact, thoughts are common, especially when first starting out. Your eyes can be open or closed and there should be nothing in your ears. When sitting in Zazen, thoughts and images might enter into your mind. These thoughts will not diminish the quality of your Zazen as long as you don't label them as good and try to hold on to them or bad and try to remove them. Instead, let thoughts come and go, don't dwell on them. Your focus should be directed inward on either counting or breathing, depending on the type of meditation that you are doing. If you feel the urge to fidget or scratch, then try to resist these urges and simply observe those feelings. The act of observing fidgety feelings rather than reacting to them will have a positive effect on your confidence.

COUNTING MEDITATION—INHALE AND EXHALE

If this is something you'd like to try, then for the first week start to count both the inhalations and exhalations of your breathing. When you inhale, focus on "one" and when you exhale focus on "two." Don't count out loud, you are only focusing your mind on the numbers to help it learn how to focus. Continue counting "three, four" and if a thought darts into your mind, simply start back at one again and continue counting.

COUNTING MEDITATION—EXHALE ONLY

When you are competent at counting on both the inhale and exhale, start to just count the exhales. Inhale, then exhale "one," then inhale and exhale "two." Focus your mind on this.

BREATHING MEDITATION

The next step is to focus on your breathing and stop counting in your head. If your mind starts to wander, be aware of it. Don't get stressed; just bring you mind back to focus on your breathing. Your mind is now doing very little and it is staying clear and empty. You are almost at the purest stage.

NATURAL BREATHING MEDITATION

This is the purest stage of Zazen meditation. To get to this stage you should be able to keep a clear mind without thoughts entering it. Once you have done this for 15 minutes, while continuing the Breathing Meditation (see above), then you are ready. With Natural Breathing, remove the focus from your breathing and just sit. To get to this stage you should be able to keep your mind clear for at least a few minutes. If you do get some thoughts, let them come and go and remain seated. Your mind should be quiet. If you start getting too many thoughts then go back to the Breathing Meditation until your mind is clear again and then proceed to Natural Breathing.

HOW LONG TO PRACTICE ZAZEN FOR

There is no strict rule for this; it really depends on your level of enthusiasm and experience. Set yourself up to succeed, so it is best to get into a regular routine. Sitting for ten minutes every day is more beneficial then sitting for 30 minutes every other day.

You might experience some aches as your body gets used to sitting in this posture for longer periods of time. If you are sitting in crossed-legged position and are not yet flexible to do full lotus, I recommend using the bed for meditation. Using a meditation cushion (or regular one) and putting that on your mattress will reduce the amount of numbness you experience in your legs. Also, placing two shoes beneath your legs to help keep the pressure off the top one, on the bottom one will also help. When meditating for more than 15 minutes, without aches and pains, you will experience stronger feelings of tranquillity. I predict this feeling will make you want to continue your Zazen experience.

I'd like to stress that you don't have to be a Buddhist to make the most of these meditation techniques. The techniques themselves do not lead to enlightenment. The purpose of spiritual meditation is to fulfill your desire for happiness. When you find happiness within, you become extremely attractive to women. Just from the simple act of meditating daily you will notice massive jumps in your confidence and women will be paying you more attention.

COMPASSION MEDITATION

Two techniques that I've found very useful for building self-esteem are Compassion Meditation and Loving Kindness Meditation. I recommend you try these as well as the traditional Zazen meditation.

Compassion Meditation will take your focus away from the "I" and toward compassion for others. We are often led to believe by society that we are all different and separate from each other. In fact, everyone has the same insecurities and worries, and we all want similar things. Compassion Meditation will help you to realize this and, in turn, your approach to anxiety will reduce because we are all in the same boat; therefore, there is nothing to fear.

PRACTICING COMPASSION MEDITATION

In meditation position, contemplate others in the world and the difficult situations they are in. Focus on how they are struggling through life and notice a feeling of compassion well up inside of you.

Do this until your mind starts to drift to other thoughts, then switch to Zazen. Bring your mind back to focus. Then, once your focus has returned, restart your Compassion Meditation.

Think about people that you know and notice your good feelings about them. It could perhaps be your parents or friends, contemplate their difficult situations. Now move on to people who you are indifferent to, people you neither dislike or like, and allow yourself to feel compassion for them. Then, finally, contemplate people you dislike. Accept that they have problems and are struggling through their lives, trying to make the best of what they have.

Stress, anger, guilt, and resentment are real things that you can carry around with you.

On several occasions I have felt stressed and then looked inside myself and asked why. In one situation a person came to mind and when I forgave that person and wished them love, the weight on my shoulders lifted. You might have a million good reasons to hate a person but it is only damaging yourself. You have to carry those bad feelings with you, so I strongly advise you let them go.

Being able to develop compassion for all people will make a huge difference to the amount of positive energy you carry inside of you. This kind of energy is incredibly attractive and will draw people to you. Why? Quite simply, you don't feel judged by them, which is a rare thing indeed.

LOVING KINDNESS MEDITATION

Loving Kindness Meditation is similar to Compassion Meditation. Try this meditation combined with Zazen and you will notice the difference in the reaction you get from people when approaching. They will literally light up when they meet you. It blew me away the first time I tried this and I have been using and teaching it ever since.

PRACTICING LOVING KINDNESS MEDITATION

Sit in the same meditative position. Start to imagine a really positive situation, perhaps a sunny day or being at the beach with friends. It can be real or imaginary; you only need to make it feel real in your mind. Who are you with? Where are you? What do you like about it?

Then imagine everybody else is smiling and really happy to see you. You talk to strangers and they all smile and fully embrace you. They love talking to you. In fact, everyone is smiling at you and is really happy to see you. Notice the feeling of love and happiness growing inside of you. Initially this feeling might only be small, but the more you meditate the bigger it will become.

Then in your mind gradually zoom out of wherever you are. Notice all the people looking up at you, waving goodbye. Notice everybody in your hometown smiling and waving at you. Notice everyone in your country smiling and full of love for you. Then notice the whole world, people from every country and nation, all happy and smiling at you. Keep that feeling inside of you.

The more you do this meditation the stronger your feeling of love will become. This will not only fill you up with good energy, but will also help remove any limiting beliefs you have about approaching.

TROUBLESHOOTING

During your Zazen meditation journey you will encounter challenges and changes. A few of the most common ones are listed below. I recommend buying a couple of books on the subject if, like me, you get very passionate about it and want to learn more.

MAKYO

Makyo are visions, hallucinations, fantasies, and revelations that can occur when practicing Zazen. Makyo can be both visual tricks of the mind or even audio tricks that could involve hearing unusual sounds. "Ma" means devil and "kyo" means the objective world. These thought processes aren't bad; they are, in fact, just tricks of the ego. The ego will try to dissuade you from doing Zazen. Your body will fight change, whether it's good or bad for you; it is just interested in keeping you alive. This is called homeostasis. Through scientific research we know that Zazen benefits us. Just be aware of these Makyo if they occur. Allow them to happen but don't assign a positive or negative emotion to them. They are meaningless and you shouldn't get discouraged or encouraged with your Zazen practice. Just continue regardless. These Makyo occur when your concentration has ripened, producing these temporary mental states. When thought waves have been calmed, past experiences and thoughts that are lodged in your deeper conscious will come to the surface sporadically. These deeper thoughts are a mixture of both the real and unreal, a bit like dreaming. Don't give any meaning to them; press on.

GOING OUT AFTER MEDITATING

When you go out the most important thing is that you start talking immediately. Being in a meditative state is great, but if you aren't talkative and you're just standing in the corner, no one is noticing. So get active, start approaching everyone whilst keeping that internal feeling of acceptance. Your first approaches will be strong and you'll be confident, but your verbal game might be a little slower. This is fine; you just need to get warmed up like any professional sports person or performer does.

Chapter 3: The Power of the Maybe

Imagine yourself as a rabbit, just living with your "rabbitness." You are not good or bad, beautiful or ugly, shy or confident. You are simply a rabbit, running around on a green hill, freely, peacefully, and without any judgments. When it is time to pass away, you do so, entering back into the mysterious space, or "God" as many call it. Through meditation you will realize that you can be happy just with yourself and by enjoying simple things. Food, water, sunlight, peace of mind, and connection with others all make me happy. When you reach this level of not needing anything to make you feel happy, then your pick-up skill will reach a new level. Any woman you approach will be aware of your happy energy and this un-neediness is a very attractive quality indeed.

Anyone who has reached the top of their game doesn't associate themselves as '"either / or" and instead just takes action. In an interview the soccer player David Beckham said, "I believe I can change the game or score a goal at any point during a match. I don't say that thinking I'm special but it is a belief that I have." Martial artist Bruce Lee once said, "You can only truly believe that you can do something if you have done it many times before."

There is a difference between beliefs and having opinions about yourself. When you do something it will train your mind to believe that you can repeat that particular action without ego attachment. There is no attachment to action and so it is the same type of belief to fix your car as it is to pick up a woman on the street. A belief goes beyond personal identification and becomes part of your subconscious mind.

Understanding that your beliefs go beyond personal identification should help you to realize that there is no point to personal identification at all. Once, after I had lined up in the grocery store, I walked toward the cashier and a woman jumped in front of me and said,

"I'm next!" I simply asked, "Is that right?" She smiled, apologized, and walked out. The cashier then told me that the woman was just playing with me. My unconscious mind would love to try to interpret and solve what just happened. Why did she play with me? Do I look like an easy target? Have other people played with me?

Instead, I simply replied with "maybe" to all of those questions in my mind. "Maybe I am an easy target, maybe I'm not, who knows?" With that acceptance of the moment the situation had no effect on me. I didn't feel embarrassed or angry.

Palm trees are the most durable of trees. When strong hurricane winds blow they can literally bend right over on to the ground, and their trunk will not snap. They are completely flexible and because of that they endure. A tree with less flexibility will simply snap or be uprooted. The "power of the maybe" enables you to be flexible like a palm tree when things start to happen around you.

The power of the maybe is at the center of ceasing personal identification with what is happening. You are not identifying with it and you are not unidentified with it. It is just an event that has happened that has no bearing on who you are.

SURRENDER AND ACTION SIDES OF THE MAYBE

The surrender side of the maybe will look something like this:

- **Her: "You're ugly." Him: "Maybe I am ugly."**
- **Her: "You look scared." Him: "Maybe I do look scared."**
- **Her: (Gives you a bad look.) Him: "Maybe I made her feel uncomfortable."**

The action side of the maybe will look more like this:

- **Her: "You're ugly." Him: "Maybe I am not ugly."**
- **Her: "You look scared." Him: "Maybe I don't look scared."**
- **Her: (Gives you a bad look.) Him: "Maybe I didn't make her feel uncomfortable."**

It is about finding balance. If you have a larger ego, feel pride, and like to control things, then try to move toward the surrender way of reacting. If you are too humble and always put others before yourself, then you will want to lean toward the action side.

MASTER THE MAYBE

You can say "the power of the maybe" out loud. I do this all the time in relationships and also during pick-up. If the woman says something negative about me, which can also be called a congruence test, I simply reply with the Surrender Side of Maybe, "Maybe that's true." I pass the test and remain completely unaffected by it. The thing that was designed to hurt me has just flown right past me and I have decided not to identify with it.

Some women like to be in control all of the time, and for similar reasons as some men do. It is probably not a good idea to get into a relationship with a controlling woman and an easy way to find out whether she is, is by using the power of the maybe. Your "Maybe that is true" response will result in a controlling woman saying something like "Yes, it definitely is true." If she has strong opinions about something that is a demonstration of being controlling, which comes from the ego. She will want to make her point final, which shows that to feel good she needs to control the situation. This is a useful test to see if a woman is a long-term prospect for you. Master the maybe and you will develop more self-confidence than you could ever have imagined.

LETTING GO

I'm sure you know people who seem to get all the breaks and appear not to experience the same troubles as most people do. They never get the flu even when everyone around them is coughing and sneezing. The right people seem to show up in their lives at the right time. They get all the luck and money always seems to turn up when they need it. It is almost as if they have a guardian angel watching over them.

What people don't realize is that this isn't luck or something that randomly happens. You attract the Tao, oneness, or God, whatever you like to call it, when you release the need to control your life. It is yours for life when a decision is made to live by letting go. Living by letting go means that you release stress, anger, worry, and fear.

PRACTICE THE ART OF LETTING GO

Start by being positive. Don't tell yourself "Just my luck" or "Things never work out for me." Instead cultivate a letting-go attitude of "I am open to allow things to just happen. I trust my luck to guide me."

When you notice yourself trying to control a situation or person, stop yourself and hold your tongue. Don't attempt to give them advice; instead, just be present and give love. Be the example and, if they need to, they will ask for help when they are ready.

No one likes to feel controlled. In a relationship a controlled woman who has been given rules will look to break those rules at the earliest opportunity she gets.

It is important for you to go on a journey of self-discovery and find out what your interests are, what your type of humor is, and what you like and dislike. This journey never stops. Your interests, personality, and humor are what you need to communicate to the woman authentically. If you find that you really enjoy shocking women with sexual directness, do it from a place of self-amusement. Everything can be good as long as it is coming from the right place.

You don't need to control anyone because you were born perfect the way you are. Things that happen that you might perceive to be bad now can turn out to be some of the greatest gifts in the future. No one knows the reason for things in the grand scheme of the universe. If a woman breaks up with you, then that could be the catalyst for you to go and achieve amazing things. In a year from now you could end up with a much hotter and more compatible girlfriend. In that case, would you not be grateful for the pain you experienced in the first break up?

Find a quiet spot in nature where no one will see or bother you. I like to take a healthy fruit and vegetable juice and go to a forest or the quiet part of my local park. Take your shoes and socks off and sit cross-legged in a state of meditation. If your mind starts to wander, then bring back your focus to your breathing again. Do this for as long as you can until your legs start to hurt. Then stretch your legs and enjoy your surroundings, maybe read a book. When you feel ready, go back to your meditative position and continue. After a stressful week I can reach a deep level of letting go after doing this for between two to three hours by repeating this pattern of meditate, rest, meditate, rest. Short meditation is great but truly letting go on a deep level can take a few hours of surrender.

After doing this your game will see dramatic improvements. If possible try a couple of approaches on the way home and notice the difference in your pick-up. If you combine this meditation, learning, and approaching regularly, you will see your pick-up skills improve very quickly.

BE LIKE WATER MY FRIEND

"Be like water my friend" – Bruce Lee

Did you know that our bodies are made up of 75 percent water and our brains 85 percent water? Think about what water is like. If it stays stationary for too long, it will become stagnant and if it is moving, it will stay clean. It does not fight against the current and instead goes with the flow. It gathers in rivers and streams and flows into the ocean until it evaporates and becomes rain again. Water doesn't intend to give life to everything on this planet; it just goes with the flow and those benefits come from it being naturally what it is.

It is natural for you to be like water, allow others to do what they want to do, and go where they want to go. Be happy to trust in the natural flow of life and treat everybody as equals. I attach no difference in value to a homeless man and a super-hot woman. We are all the same, but some are fighting and struggling and others just enjoy the ride. When you view everyone as equal you will learn to communicate with beautiful women in a much more relaxed manner.

Let go, and go with the flow. Trust that everything will work out OK in the end when you direct your focus inside. To control demonstrates a fear of loss and weakness. True power comes from surrender and, when you combine that with an ability to express yourself in a charismatic manner, the world is yours.

MASCULINE AND FEMININE POLARITIES

Knowing the differences between masculine and feminine is vitally important in your journey toward understanding yourself and improving your skills with women.

In Buddhist philosophy it is stated that the masculine is the empty, he is looking for freedom both from the body and from the mind. The feminine is the full, and she will look to retain her feeling of fullness through experiencing life and emotions.

When talking about the masculine and feminine, I'm typically referring to men and women. However, these labels are not always sufficient. Sometimes the man is more in touch with his feminine side and the woman is more in touch with her masculine side. If you are a man more in touch with his feminine side, the words below will help you to reclaim your masculine side. Through social conditioning it is very common for men to lose touch with their masculine presence.

Let me make it clear, though, women do love to date feminine men, as long as there is an underlying masculine presence. Displaying the feminine can allow you to come in under the radar when approaching a woman. For her to sleep with you, though, it is important to have a strong masculine presence and desire beneath this surface-level communication. Combining the communication channels like this is very powerful.

FREEDOM

Let's take a look at the masculine polarity in a little more detail. A man's natural urge is to be free, not trapped. The masculine will want to fight the commitment of a relationship. Commitment of any kind restricts him and prevents him from being free. When I was traveling by myself, it was probably one of the best times of my life. I recommend that every man goes out into the world by himself for a period of time to get in touch with his true, core self.

Through meditation you will be able to feel this emptiness more and more. Emptiness is not a bad thing; it is a feeling of freedom. You will still want love, safety, companionship, and sex, but it is all about balance. Meditation gets you in touch with your inner core and this will bring about a core confidence. Meditate in parallel with building a set of strong beliefs about yourself.

Imagine it like this. If your house is empty you will never worry about anyone stealing something from it. If your house is cluttered, you will always be expending energy trying to make sure everything is safe and where it should be. This is like the ego of the mind. The cluttered ego constantly needs reasons to feel satisfied. If circumstances aren't as you want them, then the ego gets affected and you react. If your mind is empty, then there is no reason to fear circumstances winding up any way other than the way they naturally do. You are completely unreactive.

RESOLUTION

A masculine man will look to resolve things to their conclusion. Within conversation the man might say something like, "OK, sorted" or "That's that then." These resolutions will allow him to be free from this conversation and move on. This is often the reason why a man will try to give a woman advice during an argument. Have you ever found yourself doing this before? I know I have. The feminine doesn't want this, though, and will look to prolong the conversation. She will want to indulge and even enhance the emotions of the conversation so she can experience it fully. As a man, the best thing you can do when an argument is happening is to be present, listen to her, and say something like "You will be OK."

DON'T REACT

If you react a lot, then you are being drawn toward the feminine and away from your masculine. When a man follows the woman and her emotions he will seem sappy or girly. If she is in a good mood, you are in a good mood; if she is in a bad mood, then you are in a bad mood. The woman will like this for a while but, soon enough, she will realize this is not how a real man behaves and look to end the relationship. You don't want to follow her emotions like this. Female emotions come and go, so don't react to them. Realize that within minutes, hours, or days these emotions will pass. They don't affect you. In any relationship you need both a masculine and a feminine. Obviously, if the woman asks for your help or it's a legitimate problem, then be there for her.

A man who is rooted in his masculine energy will be drawn toward an empty room. He will not want clutter. The feminine will want to fill every space with a pillow, candle, or decoration of some kind. She wants that feeling of fullness, which is why it's important for her to experience her full range of emotions in order to feel satisfied. She doesn't just want to feel happiness; she wants to feel sadness, anger, jealousy, love, joy, submission. Often, when she is lacking an emotion, she will find a way to get it herself.

IN THE NOW

If the man is not present with life, in the now, then the woman will look to bring him into the now so he can experience life with her. She might do this through an argument or pushing the man's buttons in some way. Your girlfriend will know how to do this very well. She will know your insecurities and pressure points better than you do. She doesn't want you to react or try to fix her, but instead just be present with her. Presence is achieved through meditation and being able to clear the mind. This stillness of the mind will wash over into the rest of your life and allow you to be present without distraction of thought. It is a lot better to offer your woman just one hour a day of your complete presence rather than five hours of distracted time.

Do your work, stay true to your purpose. If you work from home, then communicate to your partner that it is important that you aren't disturbed between certain hours. Then at the end of your working day, use your time to do things that keep your life balanced and happy. For instance, you could play tennis with your girlfriend. This is an activity where you are both completely present. A sport will give a woman a wide range of emotions too; for example, happiness, joy, frustration, anger, determination. Everything a woman does should allow her to experience emotions and, when you think about it, most things will.

If you aren't "present" during a tennis match; if, for example, your mind is on work, then your game will suffer. This is true for anything you do—work, meeting women, your relationship. Look to single-task, rather than multitask. Be fully present for the one thing that you are doing and then, when it's done, move on to the next. For men, multitasking is very inefficient and

rarely do you produce the quality you are looking for. Meditation will help you develop this single point of focus. If you find yourself getting easily distracted then write these thoughts down so you don't forget them—then continue to meditate. Ever heard a woman say men can't multitask? Well, they are right.

EMOTIONS

As a man, when you feel anger or sorrow you will probably look for ways to halt these emotions. You might think, "I'm experiencing these bad emotions, what can I do to stop them?" The feminine is the emotion, she is the fullness of life. A feminine woman will be more likely to indulge in negative emotions rather than looking for a solution to them. I found women very frustrating until I accepted this point. I could see what was wrong and so I would want to help her, but this only seemed to make things worse. As long as the woman is not actually hurting herself, then let her have her emotions and just be a rock for her.

Imagine the man is an oak tree and the woman is a squirrel. The squirrel runs around the trunk gathering the fruits of your produce. Despite the winds of life, which are life's problems, the tree might sway slightly but will never get uprooted completely. The squirrel can be vulnerable out in the open, so she needs to make sure the tree she's nested in is strong and so will test it. Don't try and trap her; instead, let her roam around you. Usually she will want to stay and not jump.

David Deangelo

THE TRAIN PICK-UP

Pick-ups usually happen in a very similar way. You approach, say something funny, build a connection, meet up again, and escalate the conversation in a clever way.

Katrina, a blonde-haired Czech woman was sitting next to me on the train. I hadn't even noticed her because I was reading a book. I remember a man on the other side of the car getting a phone call and shouting loudly. It sounded like he was talking about business and was very angry. Completely on autopilot I turned to her and said, "He sounds like he needs a bit of a cuddle." She laughed. I then noticed she had massive boobs (turned out to be EE) and a European, fashion-model face. I pressed "record" on my brain. "This is for me," I thought. I remember doing about 95 percent of the talking. She was either ignoring me or testing me. A belief that I have now is that when most women get to know me, they fall in love with me. This happens quite a lot, so I rarely care about a bit of indifference. She mentioned her age and I misheard her and thought she said 34. It then took about 10 minutes for her to actually tell me that she was 24. By that time we had got off the train and were walking down the platform together.

I remember noticing that she was making hardly any eye contact and doing very little talking, yet she was still walking close to me. I teased her on being too old for me and that she'd probably want to stay in and do the ironing while I was out partying. A bit of light qualification followed by getting her phone number just before she got on the subway. I followed up with a text message that day—"Hey crazy old Czech girl..."

When we met up again we went to a pub and then bounced to a bar a bit further down the street. During her second drink she started getting very sexual, touching my chest and my private parts, plus saying things like "Let's go and have sexy time." I thought, "This is odd, I don't have any reference points for this kind of behavior." I maintained the vibe and then took her back to my place. We kissed but then she stopped me and said, "I never do this on dates, sorry. I'm not that kind of girl." Prepared for this, I said, "You're right. We should stop." I then took her to a bar for another drink. The same groping behavior ensued, accompanied by an almost mock, Thai-girl dirty talk. We continued our drinks and I took her back to my place again. This time I managed to take her top off to reveal her firm, natural EE boobs, but, as soon as I started, I was told to stop again and that she "wasn't that kind of girl." I was fine with this but I did think it a little odd as she had been attacking my privates all evening.

I said, "No problem, that's totally cool, let's go to the park." So we went on our third date of the day. We hung out at the park and then went back to mine and this time we had sex. It turned out that a lot of guys just wanted her for her body. She liked to provoke men with her body but she would only sleep with the men who didn't get nervous. In this game it is important to be persistent. The woman is looking to see if you are man who knows what he wants or if you will be deterred at the first obstacle. I was OK with me and her not having sex. Even though she was beautiful, my life wouldn't have been any better or worse if sex had or hadn't happened. Obviously "No" means "No" but it's worth trying again when the time is right!

Chapter 4: Living with Less Is More

We live in a society that says "the more that you own, the more important you are." However, the guys who are best at the pick-up arts are the ones who live humble and straightforward lives. Their attitude is always simple: I'm a guy and she is a woman, "Hi!"

THE PURSUIT OF HAPPINESS?

Everything you add to your life brings with it an element of imprisonment. The more things you own, the more you have to protect, clean, and store. To become a true master of pick-up you must remove your attachment to all things and decrease what you already have.

We are taught from a young age that the pursuit of consumer goods is what is going to make us happy. Does it though? In my experience all it gives is short-lived gratification. What makes me happy? Among other things, peace of mind, fresh food, a purpose, the sun, human connection, and going out and using my pick-up skills to approach women; otherwise known as "sarging."

THE WEIGHT OF DEBT

Try not to get into debt or purchase outside of your means. You don't want to be approaching women as a slave; instead be a free man roaming the world. If you are thousands in debt your step will be a lot heavier and your shoulders a lot more tense than a man who is free of debt.

I live a humble life in a small studio room in a nice area of London. I don't want to ever lose that connection to earth and being real. Money is a tool that allows you to do some amazing things, but purchasing things won't make you happier.

SIMPLE LIFE V CONSUMER LIFE

The man who lives a simple life approaches the woman with nothing to lose and nothing to gain. He has nothing to gain because he is already happy in himself and simply choosing to have fun with a sexy woman. He has nothing to lose because he doesn't have an ego or think himself important.

The man who lives a consumer life approaches the woman with everything to lose and nothing to gain. He feels a level of importance and a negative reaction from the woman would destroy his personal identity. He is approaching the woman needing a positive reaction to feel good about himself. He is yet to connect to the happiness within himself and is instead in the consumer trap that has taught him that he is never enough. His neediness is apparent and consistency with women and life will always elude him.

See the pointlessness of owning anything in a world that is constantly in the process of death and new life. At a point in the future everyone on this planet will die and everything you have ever owned will be destroyed. This could be due to an asteroid or a planetary event, but it will happen. We don't actually ever own anything. Money is a currency that we currently use, but even that is becoming less physical and more computer based. Maybe one day our financial transactions will only be made by a card. How much power will we be giving to those private institutions when they can quite easily just close our account and stop our card from working? They would have control over us and we would be completely reliant on them. Choose to remain as free as possible, just how you came into this world.

Pick three things of importance that you own and give them away. The more important they are, the better you will feel when you give them away and sever your attachment to them.

THE POWER OF EMOTIONS

In 1971 three physiotherapists produced a study on muscle testing; they found that muscles would become weak when the body was exposed to negative external events. For instance, patients would hold a small weight in their hand and have it outstretched. They would then be shown images of war and famine on a projector. On viewing these nasty images, their arm would instantly go weak and they would want to drop the weight. Conversely, they discovered that giving the patients positive stimuli would cause their muscles to become strong. These findings led to noticing patterns in the average life expectancy of people in a positive state of mind and those in a negative state of mind. The patients with positive emotions would live significantly longer, several years more, in fact, than those consumed by negative feelings and emotions.

Dr. J. Diamond, a psychiatrist used muscle testing to diagnose and test for psychiatric problems in patients. He developed the test further so it became a two-people procedure. The first person is the "tested" and he or she would hold out their arm parallel to the ground. The second person would then hold the first person's wrist and then push down on it while telling person one to "resist" this. A resistance test. A statement would be made to person one and if the statement was negative or false the arm would go weak. If the statement was true or positive, then the arm would stay strong. The subject was also asked to visualize both positive and negative things in his mind. For instance, the image of Adolf Hitler would cause the arm to drop to the floor and the image of Mother Teresa would result in the arm becoming stronger. They began to classify emotions into different levels of weakness and strength depending on how the subjects reacted during testing.

The point of weakness within the body comes below the level 200. This is very counter intutitve because common knowledge suggests that anger is strength, but this only registers at level 150. Notice that the greatest fighters will enter combat in relaxed states; these register in the higher levels. You will see this in most martial arts; a clear mind and relaxed state allows you to be stronger and make better decisions.

When approaching you want to cultivate the higher levels which will lead you to power and strength. The first step, the approach, will be courage, doing something that scares you but you do it anyway. If you are in a state of fear of talking to women, then this will lead to desire "wanting to make the approach" and then this desire will lead to anger. This anger can be a force to drive you to reach the level of courage. "I'm fed up of this average life, I want something better!!" and make the approach. During my day I mostly function between the Reason and Love levels 400–500. If I do a long meditation session on a good day, I can reach 600. Teaching over 1,000 students face to face, I've found that the ones that do best on boot camp have willingness, acceptance, and a reason for attending the course. They

don't question things too much and try everything with a positive attitude. These students will get the most numbers, kisses, and full closes over the weekend.

Some might have had really tough past experiences and be operating on the level of fear or lower. The desire to get success with women could lead to anger about why there isn't an abundance of options already and this can lead to courage to take the boot camp. Courage is the starting point to reaching the higher levels and the path to success. It is important to reach courage and avoid the state of pride. Pride is ego and will result in justifications and reasons why there is no need to take action. People with large egos are stronger than those consumed by fear but will always be trapped at this stage and miss out on real power and strength. You might notice that people with ego or pride need to dominate the weaker to continue to feel good and operate at this level. True power is truth and self-sustained.

Notice that your best results come when operating at the higher levels. If you can reach the level of Joy while approaching, crazy things will happen. Every woman will be eager to meet you and everything you say will be perfect. These times will result in multiple kiss closes and having a choice of which woman or women you want to take home that night. The higher levels are addictive and once you've experienced a night like this you will want more. Everything else will seem so low and pointless compared to these feelings.

Through regular meditation you will cultivate an inner awareness where you will be able to recognize how you are feeling. If you notice you are operating on a lower level, then accept that emotion and continue to take action—"action is on the level of courage." By doing this you will give yourself the best chance to turn it around and have a great day.

The level of love is a fantastic starting point to focus on. Begin wishing everyone love, the people you like, and even the ones you don't like. Do this in your daily life and wish people you meet during the day love as well. This will cause you to rise up the levels and lead to big positive shifts in your pick-up skills.

THE THREE CORNERS OF HAPPINESS

If you are feeling happy, then inevitably you will make others around you feel happy too. People gravitate toward people who make them feel good. This human hardwiring keeps us alive—moving toward things that give us good emotions and moving away from things that give us bad emotions. This is the first corner of happiness and is your sensory experience of the earth.

FIRST CORNER

Too often, through the avoidance of negative emotions, people become indifferent. They are OK with where they are, not approaching women, and so don't take any risks. Maybe a woman could reject you and this negative emotion is something that you want to avoid. In doing so, though, you are shutting down part of your life and this stagnation will slowly rot you down over time. Realize that sometimes a little pain will result in greater pleasure over the long term. Realizations like this are one of the core benefits of the mind.

Your experiences of pleasure and pain on the psychological level are a lot more powerful than on the physical level. For example, if you are in a nice setting with nice people but internally you are stressed, it can be very difficult. Alternatively, if you are in a not-so-nice setting but internally you feel happy, then life is good. In fact, it could be raining and cold, but, if you feel happy, you'll tend not to focus on any physical limitations.

SECOND CORNER

The second corner of happiness comes through removing distracting mental noise. As a man, acquiring freedom will often lead to great happiness. Seeing the world clearly, without the mind polluting your perception, helps with this. Meditation is the tool used for removing this distracting noise and for taming the emotions that come with it.

Many people, myself included, believe happiness is a default state of mind. When all the clutter and mental limitations have been removed you can start to feel peace and a long-lasting glow of happiness.

THIRD CORNER

The third thing to bear in mind is that humans have a set of common needs. For the last couple of years, teaching dating full time, I have found consistent happiness comes when the following are in place:

MASLOW'S HIERARCHY OF HUMAN NEEDS

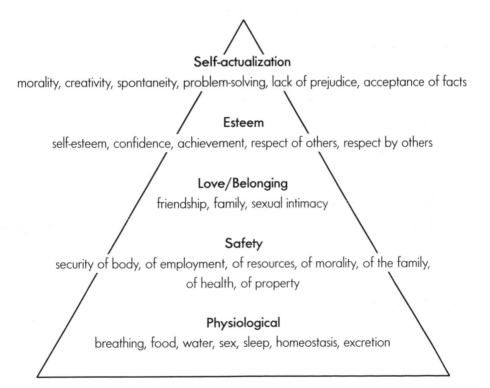

Self-actualization
morality, creativity, spontaneity, problem-solving, lack of prejudice, acceptance of facts

Esteem
self-esteem, confidence, achievement, respect of others, respect by others

Love/Belonging
friendship, family, sexual intimacy

Safety
security of body, of employment, of resources, of morality, of the family, of health, of property

Physiological
breathing, food, water, sex, sleep, homeostasis, excretion

If you aren't happy, then probably one of the needs in the diagram on the previous page is missing. Take some time and look at your life. Is it in balance? Personally, working from home has meant that I need to be more pro-active in the love and belonging section, making sure I see friends and family regularly and nurturing those connections. A day with no social contact can make me feel unhappy. If friends aren't around, I will go out and give a stranger a cuddle.

BE HARSH WITH YOURSELF

A positive man can recognize his faults, but he is also aware that he is made up of a lot of other parts too. The negative man is unable to do this. It is important that you remove the all-or-nothing mindset. You are not great or awful at the present moment; instead maybe something specific isn't going that well but the rest of you is positive.

For instance, the positive man might say, "I wasn't very good at approaching yesterday, I'll have to spend more time working on that." The negative man is more likely to say something like, "I sucked yesterday, I scared every woman that I approached."

The difference is that the negative man is critical of himself as a whole, whereas the positive man is just critical of one specific thing. This way the positive man stays happy and confident and the negative man loses all faith in himself and starts to feel terrible.

EXERCISE: LIMITATIONS AND QUALITIES

List your top 10 limitations and then your top 10 qualities. The more that you can list the better. Remember, when you are out don't be harsh on yourself as a person, just focus on the specific thing that you did wrong. Doing this exercise will help you to realize that you are made up of many different parts.

HAVING THAT GOOD FEELING

It is important to remember that the words are always secondary to the underlying feeling of an interaction. One study from the University of California states that: "Up to 93 percent of communication effectiveness is determined by nonverbal cues." This was broken down into:

38%—Voice tonality

55%—Facial expression and energy

7%—The words used

Obviously, words can be important but the main thing to do is to concentrate on keeping that good feeling inside of your body. This feeling can be achieved by following the three corners previously mentioned on happiness (see pages 76–78). Also, talking to a lot of women is fundamental and will help you to relax during future interactions.

FIND WAYS TO STAY FEELING GOOD

A lot of the guys who are naturally good with women recognize what energy women respond best to. They notice that when they are feeling good, full of energy, and are giving out positive vibes, women tend to respond better to them. Usually this is a subconscious realization ("When I'm like this, women like me more") and so they look to enter this state as much as possible.

PHYSIOLOGY

The best guys with women will find ways to make themselves feel happy and positive. Externally they might do things to their physiology to help put themselves into this state. Examples of this are:

- **Talk loudly**
- **Sing**
- **Don't be afraid to take up space**
- **Be physically dominant**
- **Smile**
- **Laugh**
- **Do things that amuse themselves**
- **Talk to a stranger**
- **High-five**
- **Jump**
- **Walk in a cool way**
- **Look around and engage with the environment**

POSITIVE MENTAL PROCESSES

A guy who is good with women will have positive mental processes. Two guys can look very similar physically, but without even talking to them you can tell who is the more attractive.

The guy who is playing negative thoughts in his head—stress, worry, anger—will be putting out a negative presence. His energy will have receded into the back of his mind and he will appear passive and anxious. The guy who is positive and engaging with his environment will have a completely different energy. He will be proactive, looking around, internally happy, and completely removed from people's opinions. He will be a much more attractive person.

Examples of these positive mental processes are:

- **Notice everything cool about the current moment**
- **Rationalize everything as positive**
- **Never let a negative thought enter your brain**
- **Realize that everyone else is worried about what you think of them**
- **Play funny or positive mental thought loops in your mind**
- **Have an empty mind**

I used to be negative and this came out in passive aggression. By rewiring my brain to rationalize everything as positive, my confidence exploded. I now constantly notice all the cool things about the present moment:

- **"She looks brilliant"**
- **"I like her outfit"**
- **"He's a cool guy"**
- **"She'd look amazing in a bikini"**
- **"I'm loving the sun today"**
- **"That grandma has a funky walk"**
- **"I like that dude's shoes"**
- **"Wow, they sell green drinks, I'm going to try one"**
- **"She wants me"**
- **"Those women can't wait to meet me, look how bored they are"**
- **"That was cool, I even approached, most people wouldn't"**
- **"I bet I can add value to those women"**

Nowadays it is very difficult for me to feel depressed as I only ever want to feel happy and positive. If you are making a change in your life you will find that you revert back to your old behaviors from time to time. However, as long as you maintain your awareness and are able to notice this, you can start being proactively positive again. Meditation helps a lot with expanding your awareness by creating distance from your mind. The ideal is to have a positive, fun, happy mind with daily periods of mind emptiness.

CARRY YOURSELF WITH PRIDE

I cannot stress enough how important it is to have good posture. I realized this through reading about it in books and from an experience with a friend.

One day I was having coffee with my friend Chloe, who is a typical high self-esteem model type. She told me that I should sit up straight. I thought she was being cheeky and treated it like a test. My response was something like "Cool," demonstrating that I wasn't affected by the remark. However, her comment gave me a second of clarity and I started noticing the way other people were sitting while drinking their coffee. Chloe was bolt upright, head high, and spine straight. As I looked around I could see that some people's posture was OK, while others had terrible posture. What I was able to tell instantly through my years of infield experience was how much people loved themselves just by the way they were sitting. Instantly, I fixed my posture and set myself a 30-day challenge of only sitting with a straight back and hitting myself every time I slouched. This probably wasn't the most humane way to fix a posture problem, but I did quickly begin to associate pain with slouching. Problem solved. Since then I've spent a lot of time researching yoga and core-strengthening exercises. I recommend that you check out www.yogagarden.jp, which has an excellent collection of free videos that contain advice on this subject.

Chapter 5: Stop the Thought Tree From Taking Root

As humans we like to think that we are free-thinking and in complete control of our lives. However, just a couple of minutes in meditation makes it clear to us that this is not the case. Thinking too much during a pick-up is bad and you usually end up tripping over your own feet. The best naturals and guys who do great with women don't think at all.

BOOT CAMP EXAMPLE

At a recent boot camp I was taking a student through meditation and I recognized that he was a very analytical man. We sat down and just concentrated on our own breathing. I told him to tell me whenever a thought came into his mind and what the thought was. After two seconds passed the first thought entered his head.

"The grain on this wooden table looks like a fox."

I acknowledged this and then I explained that I just wanted him to sit there and focus on his breathing. I wanted him to have a clear mind. We started again. A couple of seconds later he noticed that he was having another thought.

"The white circle on the table looks like a moon on Jupiter."

He confessed that he felt he must be pretty crazy if he couldn't sit still for just a couple of minutes without a thought entering his mind. However, he certainly isn't alone in this; the majority of the world's population is the same.

THOUGHT TREES

Having a lot of negative thoughts running around in your head is especially bad for pick-up. These thoughts are triggered by events in the environment. Something will happen in your environment and the mind will then look to interpret what it means. This will then create a chain-thought tree, where one thought links to another and then another, until you become aware of what is happening and stop the process. Thought trees are bad because you will start to overthink things which will expend a lot of your energy, plus the thoughts may be negative ones which will create a negative energy in you.

Here's an example of a thought tree:

"That's a hot woman" > "I like her boobs" > "She is with another woman" > "I don't feel comfortable talking to two women" > "I got rejected once by those two mean girls at school" > "I hated Sophie and Laura" > "I had a bad time at school" > "Why couldn't I make friends at school?" > "Maybe there is something wrong with me" > "Tristan thought there was something wrong with me" > "Why did I add him on Facebook?"

Thought trees will go on and on. Within the space of a few seconds you will have gone from feeling confident and happy to probably hating yourself. Negative energy will then ooze out of you, repelling all the women in your path until you get a good response. A positive response will give you some positive thoughts until the next bad event happens. In pick-up bad events are very common because you are outside of your comfort zone and opening yourself up to weird social situations.

The brilliance of meditation is that it allows you to catch the first thought and stop the chain reaction happening. Meditation gives you awareness, or the mind's eye. You will get thoughts as you walk through a bar or a club; they're inevitable. However, with practice, you will be able to control them and not let them affect your night.

HOW TO NURTURE A STRONG POSITIVE OUTLOOK

When I first started meditating I asked myself why I was doing it. A lot of other guys who are good with women don't have to. I soon realized that a lot of these men had to get drunk before making their approach, which shuts down the thinking part of the brain. It also makes you erratic and socially un-calibrated, but it does stop you overthinking. When you are drunk you just do, and don't think. With alcohol you can reach a sweet spot of drinking; just enough to turn off the analytical side of your brain and not so much that you appear drunk. However, this sweet spot doesn't usually last long and as soon as you go over the edge there is no coming back. It demonstrates that there is a lot of value in approaching women sober because it shows that you have real confidence.

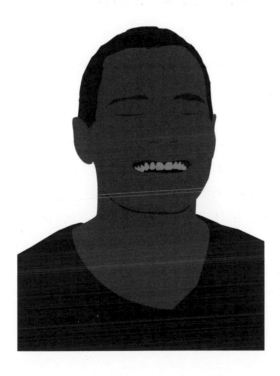

Women like men to be happy, confident, positive, dominant, and fun. If you start to think things like...

- **"Should I kiss the woman?"**
- **"She gave me a funny look."**
- **"I'm not in a good state right now."**
- **"What was my pick-up line?"**

... the interaction will inevitably fall flat because: A—you are trying; and B—your thought loops will self-sabotage your state.

EVERYTHING IS A POSITIVE

I did notice some naturals who were very good with women and didn't need alcohol or drugs. Even in difficult situations where the social interaction was going against them they didn't lose their confidence. I realized that this was because they attached very few negative meanings to anything. In fact, everything that happened was positive.

An example of this that springs to mind happened to my instructor Cupid on a recent boot camp. We were sitting down in a bar with the Hot Babe (HB) Helper and the students were taking it in turns to practice their conversation skills on her. This activity sees massive student growth because as instructors we get to hear and see everything and can make instant tweaks. Toward the end of the session one of the students started trying to tease Cupid by saying to the HB Helper, "Have you met my friend Cupid? He doesn't talk much. How's it going, man?" The student held out his hand to shake Cupid's hand but pulled it away at the last second. "He's quite slow, isn't he? Must be that big belly."

The usual response to this kind of onslaught would be for the person to think to themselves, "What does this mean?" and then to find a list of reasons why it is him being attacked. Cupid did think, "What does this mean?" and he came up with the reason that it was funny and was genuinely laughing at this guy trying to win his approval.

GOOD FEELINGS

Always remember to ask yourself, "What is great about now?" Use those empowering words that we talked about in the section on positive mental processes (see pages 80–81) to maximize your good feelings. There will be certain negative triggers that you react most to and it is important that you identify these. With meditation you will become a lot more aware and so this task will become easier. When you are out and you notice that you are suddenly feeling stressed, anxious, or unhappy, ask yourself why. "What has just happened to make me feel like this?" When you can identify the triggers, you can remove them.

You can remove a trigger by changing your state during it. For example, if a friend canceling on you gives you lots of negative thoughts you will want to:

- **Stop the thought tree from happening, so stop your mind after thought one.**
- **Give yourself a positive reason why this is OK. "This gives me time to solo sarge."**
- **Change your state, so sing, jump up and down, and laugh to change your association to this event.**

I do realize this can be quite tricky, but if you take the time to do this the results will astound you within just a few proactive days .

IMPLEMENTATION TASK: POSITIVITY CHALLENGE

During your next five sarges open 10 sets per sarge and only allow yourself to have positive thoughts. If you start to indulge in negative thoughts and don't catch the first one, then you must start over at sarge one. Complete this task successfully by carrying out five positive-thought-only sarges in a row. For example, if a woman rejects you, then it's brilliant because you approached in the first place; if your wing is doing better than you, then that is fantastic because you are hanging with a great guy. This is a tough mission but a vitally important one. I know you are up to it, best of luck!

WHAT IS THIS SELF-ESTEEM CHITCHAT ALL ABOUT?

There is an excellent definition of self-esteem in the book *Beat Low Self-Esteem with CBT:* "Self-esteem is a measurement based on our own or others criteria of what is good." Low self-esteem tends to stem from childhood, even if a child grew up in a happy environment. Sometimes parents encourage a child but in the wrong way. This creates a negative core belief that shapes the child's life. We all like to think that we are in control of our lives, but this is not the case. Unless you gain awareness of your core beliefs you will end up reacting to the same things over and over again. You develop circular behavior patterns that hold you back and influence what you do day to day and we aren't even aware that it is happening.

THE LAYERS OF SELF-ESTEEM

Your self-esteem has a triangular structure. Your day-to-day thoughts are at the top, your processing mind that asks questions is in the middle, and your core beliefs that you have developed over time are at the bottom.

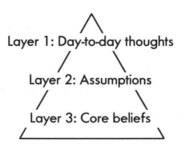

Layer 1: Day-to-day thoughts

Layer 2: Assumptions

Layer 3: Core beliefs

Let's say you notice Brad Pitt wearing a cool white shirt in a celebrity magazine. The shirt looks good on him, he's a cool guy, so you decide to buy it for yourself. You walk out of the store wearing your brand-new shirt, and you feel good. I believe walk was the wrong word there; you swagger out of the store—the confidence is oozing out of you.

How long will this happy feeling last? Will the shirt continue to make you feel confident and attractive in a month's time? What if you see another picture of David Beckham wearing a different shirt? What if one of your underlying core beliefs is that you are ugly?

Well, this feeling can last minutes, a few days, or a maximum of a couple of weeks. Fairly soon the shirt will begin to lose its power and then you will start to look to buy another one. You must learn to love yourself rather than trying to cover up a lack of self-love through consumer purchases which never last.

Layer 1: Day-to-day thought
"I love my new shirt."

Layer 2: Assumption
"If I wear this shirt, then I will be attractive."

Layer 3: Core belief
"I'm ugly."

This is the classic consumer trap of making you feel like you are never enough. This is often how brands market themselves. Instead, by locating and changing negative core beliefs you can feel like that million-dollar man all of the time. Wearing the shirt will work for a while, but as soon as you make a negative assumption about yourself in the shirt, it will cease to work.

MY NEGATIVE CORE BELIEFS

One of my main negative core beliefs was that "I'm not good enough as I am." This negative belief was formed during my childhood, despite my parents being friendly, hardworking, lovely people. After completing something I'd never get a "well done" or "that's excellent work." Instead, as encouragement, I was told to "do better next time" or "that's not good enough, let me show you."

Often times my mum would do my homework for me and I'd just sit and watch. Let me please stress that my mum is great and she only wanted the best for me; she wanted me to achieve. I truly believe this. However, the vast majority of people aren't psychologists or pick-up artists, so they don't understand about the knock-on effects that things can have.

This negative core belief drove me to be the best at everything in the hope I could get some recognition or at least avoid feeling bad. However, it is never possible to be the best at everything all of the time.

This core belief is probably the reason why I'm writing in the library now at 11 p.m. and not being a cool guy and just chilling. The negative aspect of having this core belief was that I'd beat myself up all of the time. Any interaction that wasn't perfect, a woman canceling on me, and comparing myself to other people, constantly got me down. I'd literally be stressed out and passive aggressive all of the time. I'd achieved a lot in comparison to my friends, but I wasn't happy and I'd feel like people could see into my unhappiness. Being happy would be momentary, often induced through alcohol. I have now softened this core belief so that I don't beat myself up, and instead love myself. I do still work long hours but this is because I choose to and not because of some automatic process I'm running.

GET YOUR SELF-ESTEEM IN ORDER

When you get your three layers of self-esteem in order you can become ridiculously happy and cool. Only yesterday I was sitting down by the river in the sun reading and I got "opened" by an old man. Score! He asked me where a certain street was. We had a short chat, during which he said, "What do you do?"

"A life coach," I replied.

He said, "Ah yes, I can see that, you have an aura about you. I think you are probably a very good life coach."

Needless to say that put a smile on my face.

A couple of hours later, a woman walking her child home from school said to me, "Nice weather today isn't it?"

I replied with, "Yes, it's fantastic!"

She then said, "No, you are fantastic!" I was confused and she repeated herself and said, "You're fantastic, you're like a movie star."

Let me mention that I was wearing sweatpants, and that I don't think my looks are on a movie-star level. The woman was drawn to my energy, positivity, and self-esteem; that is what "good-looking" really is. Good-looking is your energy and attitude; truly remember this. I understood this on a deep level a couple of years ago. I was doing really well in a nightclub, women were staring at me, and I was getting numbers and kisses all over the place. I then remember going to the restroom toward the end of the night and looking in the mirror. To my shock my hair was terrible, plus I had a massive zit on my nose. However, inside my head I was thinking that I was the coolest, most attractive guy in the nightclub. That was a big "a-ha" moment.

Getting your core beliefs and assumptions in order allows you to literally become a people magnet. Changing your day-to-day thoughts is useful but it will only create temporary highs. Thoughts will enter into your head due to noticing events happening around you. In fact, if you don't meditate, they will come into your head all of the time. You will be completely out of control if you don't meditate. When a thought enters your head, instantly your brain will make an assumption about the situation, "What does this mean?" Your brain will then look at your core beliefs and give you back an answer.

As mentioned previously, core beliefs are the bottom layer of our thinking. They can be both positive and negative. We consider these beliefs to be true and it is rare that we ever question them. These beliefs then form the base on which we live our lives. Often, in the case of low self-esteem, you will find many negative core beliefs.

Low self-esteem can be caused by a succession of failures or having been undermined as a child and told you weren't good enough. If you get told that you can't do something enough times, you will believe it. Then, as you get older, you will look to collect more evidence to support this belief. In fact, as humans we are always trying to confirm our own personal identity and behave congruently to it.

A lot of us make affirmations but they seldom work in the long term. A temporary boost is possible, but within just a few minutes their effect tends to wear off. Why do you think this is? Well, the reason for this is that our thoughts won't make much difference if they are in direct contradiction with our core beliefs. For example, if you say to yourself "I am confident" but one of your core beliefs is "I'm never enough," then you will not be confident. The thought you have created is not a fact to your mind and so will be labeled as rubbish and thrown out.

Let's look at an example that illustrates how self-esteem operates on an automatic level. A man is sitting on a park bench and a woman stares at him as she cycles past. Here are two reactions to this situation:

REACTION 1

Layer 1: Day-to-day thought

"She is staring at me."

Layer 2: Assumption

"Maybe I gave her a weird look."

Layer 3: Core belief

"I'm never good enough."

REACTION 2

Layer 1: Day-to-day thought

"She is staring at me."

Layer 2: Assumption

"She wants to meet me."

Layer 3: Core belief

"I am an attractive person."

You see how the facts don't change? A woman is looking at you as you sit on a park bench but the two different reactions are drastically different. The second reaction is driven by having a positive assumption about the situation. Your thoughts and assumptions are driven by your core beliefs and behavior. If one of your core beliefs is that you doubt yourself, then you are more likely to be a negative person. That is why it is so important to stay positive throughout the day. Train yourself to do this and even without using any of the techniques given here your core beliefs will improve automatically over time.

If you force yourself to be positive, then you will be more likely to do new things and so give yourself more positive reference experiences. These reference experiences are usually going to be things outside of your comfort zone. The more of these you get, then the faster your core beliefs will change to positive ones. "I'm never good enough" will soon turn into "I'm good enough sometimes" and this will turn into "I'm mostly good enough." When your core beliefs change a whole new world of opportunities opens up to you. You will find that you are able to communicate with people you used to perceive as high value. Going for a new promotion at work or performing in front of big groups of people becomes a lot easier.

Personally, I noticed that I used to make assumptions based on limiting core beliefs rather than facts about the situation. It is important to maintain awareness and challenge all of your beliefs with facts. "Why am I never good enough?" "Have there been times when I have been good enough?" "Am I good enough at least some of the time?" The majority of the time a core belief will not be based on a fact but instead on your opinion or someone else's opinion of you.

EXERCISE: IDENTIFYING MY NEGATIVE CORE BELIEFS

Take a few minutes to think, then write down some limiting core beliefs that you have. Be brutally honest with yourself. You might feel a few negative emotions when doing this but it's vitally important to sorting out your inner game. Next to each core belief, write down a score between 1 and 20 to show how strongly you believe it at the moment, 1 being "I don't really believe this at all." and 20 being "This is definitely true." We will return to this exercise later on in the book to see if they have positively changed.

KNOW WHEN YOU'RE WINNING

Low self-esteem is often caused by people being overly harsh on themselves. We all have rules for ourselves about what standards we need to reach to be happy. A lot of these standards are excessively high, especially those set by people studying self-help material. Most of the time people don't even know what "good" means when talking about picking up women. Some men think that getting every woman is the only successful outcome. Do you think that needing to pick up every woman in order to feel happy is a sensible aim on which to base your self-esteem?

The reason that the self-help community has a lot of perfectionists in it is that in order to improve yourself you have to have goals and dream big. This will then make you feel bad for not having those things and push you across, as Tony Robbins, self-help author and motivational speaker, likes to call it, the "indifference threshold." This pain causes you to take action and sets you on your path to making your dreams a reality.

QUEST FOR PERFECTION

The downside to the quest for pick-up perfection is that if the interaction isn't flawless or you don't get the best response, you will beat yourself up about it. This definitely isn't healthy thinking and is one of the quickest ways to destroy your self-esteem. Having negative thoughts and blaming yourself after you get rejected by a woman will only lessen your chances of improving this area of your life. Instead, lower your standards. Define success as just opening and trying out a new technique. Anything else that happens doesn't matter. Just open and then give yourself a massive pat on the back afterward. This can be easier said than done and so if you are struggling to make this transition, then a boot camp will fix this.

There was a small grocery store in my street where I used to live and every day I would notice that the man who worked in there was really happy. He always had a massive smile on his face and he greeted everyone warmly. However, some of the customers were difficult and would give him a hard time. They'd come into the store and mock and tease him. I always felt sorry for him but he never seemed to feel sorry for himself. In fact, he didn't seem to mind at all. This drove me crazy because I couldn't understand how someone so much worse off than me could be so much happier than I was. So one day I decided to ask him why he was always so happy. He replied, "I'm alive." His rule for feeling happy was simple—"If I'm alive, then that's fantastic!"

MISSION ACHIEVABLE

You don't want people to walk all over you and not achieve anything in your life, but at the same time you need to maintain your confidence and self-esteem. The best way to do this is by setting yourself small achievable missions each night that you go out. For example, talk to three women you've never met before. If you do this, then that's brilliant and anything on top of this is an excellent bonus. If you are new or even at an intermediate level, then threesomes, strippers, and hot women shouldn't be your criteria for feeling happy. If they are, then you will never feel happy and these kinds of women easily pick up on this stuff and are repelled by it. Don't get caught in a never-ending, self-defeating loop of doom. It's OK to fail or do something wrong.

EXERCISE: THE PERFECTIONIST EXERCISE

PART ONE

Make a list of all the areas that you feel you need to be perfect in. Here are a few examples:

- **"Other people will think less of me if I make a mistake."**
- **"If a woman rejects me, then that is a failure."**
- **"I must be able to pick up every night."**

PART TWO

Now write down where you think these perfectionist views have come from. What parts of your past have shaped you to take on these core beliefs? Then below each one, list all the reasons why keeping these beliefs is beneficial to you, if it actually is. Then write all the reasons why these perfectionist views are holding you back. After doing this exercise you will have started the subconscious process of challenging these views, which is the first step to removing them for good.

WHO AM I?

As strange as it sounds, you really aren't who you might think you are. The image that we have of ourselves, whatever it may be, is not real.

Students often ask me if I was a natural before learning about pick-up. I understand why they would ask such a question. I used to ask the same question several years ago. The answer is no, but this isn't as straightforward a question to answer as you might think.

In the book *How to See Yourself As You Really Are* by the Dalai Lama, he talks about the "I" that feels so real in the mind, the life story, is inherently fake. The "I" in our minds is nothing but a figment of our imagination.

For example, suppose you fail to approach a beautiful woman in the street. You might say something like "I'm such a loser" or perhaps something a little less extreme such as "I should've approached her." Now how does the "I" appear in your mind during that moment? How does this "I" that our whole lives are lived through seem to exist? By taking a minute to reflect on questions like these you will start to reveal that the mind's "I" and "you" are actually

different. Notice that when you get angry with yourself you are getting angry with your mind. "I can't believe I did that." The mind that is angry and the mind that you are angry with appear to be different. Crazy huh?

So when I'm asked was I a natural before, if I say no then I create this fake "I" of not being good with women. This identity will feel very real and I will immediately start to live in alignment with it. A core human need is to act congruently with how a person perceives themselves. So by saying "I wasn't a natural" I create an identity out of it and I will then start to take on this fake identity. My behavior will become passive and weak and I will begin to mimic somebody who is not good with women.

When you are living in the present moment, outside of your mind, you have no self-image or "I," you just are. Words are abstract in essence; they don't really mean anything. So you can say what you will, just remember not to create an identity out of them. Your mind and your ego will love it if you do.

Things that have happened in the past could have shaped our current behavior and beliefs but they don't make us who we are. Who we are comes from an understanding that we are separate from our minds. This becomes clearer through reflection and meditation. Who we are is not "I'm a computer programmer" or "I'm a nice person." Instead it is a realization, an understanding.

Good or bad events that have happened in your life are just things that happened—they don't have any basis in determining who you are. Let go of negative excuses as the reasons why you behave the way you do. Maybe your parents weren't as supportive as they could have been but that is their issue, not yours. Take responsibility for shaping your behavior and character yourself. It is not cool to be a fully grown adult and to blame others for your problems. This is the same for the common problem of having a bad family upbringing. "I'm like this because my mum was always stressed around me." This once again is a fake image in the mind of the "I". Let go of this, and limiting behaviors can be fixed. You as an adult are solely responsible for what you do.

It is OK to have beliefs about yourself; just don't focus on them too much. Just like having thoughts is absolutely fine; in fact, positive ones should be encouraged. As long as there is the acceptance that they are only thoughts and have no bearing on actual reality.

You don't have to reach enlightenment to achieve a better understanding of who you are. Begin today by carrying out the reflection meditation tasks below. It should only take a few minutes to do each one. Over time your understanding of yourself will increase. Being able to distinguish that you are not your mind is the first step. Take the time to carry out these four reflective meditations as often as you can. Ideally you want to meditate for 20 minutes a day, as well as a ten-minute self-esteem meditation once a week. The more you meditate, the quicker you will see improved results.

IMPLEMENTATION TASK: REFLECTIVE MEDITATION

- Remember a time when you were annoyed with yourself; for example, perhaps you were late for a meeting.

1. How did the "I" appear to you in your mind at that time?
2. How were you holding on to that "I" mentally?
3. Notice how the "I" appears to stand alone, its own character.

- Remember a time when you were annoyed with a part of your body; for example, your hair.

1. How did the "I" appear to you in your mind that time?
2. How were you holding on to that "I" mentally?
3. Notice how the "I" appears to stand alone, its own character.

- Remember a time when you did something awful and thought "I shouldn't have done that."

1. How did the "I" appear to you in your mind that time?
2. How were you holding on to that "I" mentally?
3. Notice how the "I" appears to stand alone, its own character.

- Remember a time when you did something brilliant and you were very proud of it.

1. How did the "I" appear to you in your mind that time?
2. How were you holding on to that "I" mentally?
3. Notice how the "I" appears to stand alone, its own character.

Chapter 6:
Stop Pushing My Buttons

Your emotional buttons are your emotional reactions. If someone pushes them, then you react in a certain way. Always ask the question, "who has control over the way I react to my buttons, me or you?"

Things used to really get my goat, annoy me, tick me off, you get me? One of the things that really used to annoy me was when a friend was my "wing" (see page 9) and they didn't approach when we were out. I'd get annoyed that we should be taking it in turns to approach and that he wasn't offering any value. I'd encourage, beg, or get angry. I knew I should be talking to women and I would get frustrated that I wasn't making progress. My thinking was that we are out together and so we should be approaching together.

I'd often say things like, "You not approaching is putting me in a bad state." My friend would correct me, saying, "Who is in control of your state? Me or you?" This really resonated with me and I had a moment of realization: I'm the only one in control of my own state and my own "buttons." David DeAngelo's DVD set *Man Transformation* also talks about this. For somebody to get a reaction out of you or press your buttons you have to let them do this.

Anyone close to you, but particularly your girlfriend or mum, will know exactly what your buttons are. So it is important to:

- **Recognize what they are.**
- **Maintain awareness and keep control of them.**
- **Take steps to remove them—this comes through awareness and staying in the moment; mentally making the decision not to react; and changing your associations in the moment—do something fun to change your state.**

Remember that you are solely in control of your own state and your own buttons. There are some state changes that are needed for healthy survival. For instance, if you are unhappy that your friend is doing a lot better than you are in his career, this can actually be a useful emotion as it will give you motivation to take action. Button fixing is for your relationships and for when you're out meeting people.

When I was getting frustrated with my friend, really I was getting frustrated with myself. Deep down I was annoyed that I couldn't approach on my own. I took action. Now, when I go out with my friends they know that I have to be social to keep my skills sharp. I usually spend some time away from them doing solo sarging and I will also talk to new people in front of them. That old button that I had doesn't exist anymore.

As you modify your thinking you will start to experience some fantastic dramatic changes. Realize that you are completely responsible for how you are feeling at any one time. As soon as you realize this, others will cease to have any power or control over you.

Whenever you have a time where you get taken away from your center, take a moment to look inside yourself and see what is happening. Directing your focus inward allows you to permit the flow of inner activity without judgment or attachment. In time this cultivation of self-mastery, self-acceptance, and self-awareness will diminish the reaction you can have to nothing. If you don't start to direct your focus inward, then the same patterns of event and reaction will repeat themselves forever.

IMPLEMENTATION TASK: BUTTON AWARENESS

This week, as well as doing your daily meditation, monitor your state when you are out sarging. Notice when somebody else changes your state or annoys you. Make a note of it on your phone and then follow the steps above to remove it. Remember you are the only one in control of yourself.

PAIN BODIES

In the book *A New Earth,* Eckhart Tolle states that a pain body is a negative energy field that is trapped inside your inner being. In my experience, most people carry pain bodies inside of them. Bear with me here and let me explain. A pain body exists because something happened in the past, usually a bad childhood experience. This experience manifests itself into your neural pathways in the form of bad energy.

Classic victim mentality is to believe that the past is more important than the present. The opposite of this is the actual truth. An event might happen in your surrounding environment that will cause you to retreat into your mind. If the event links to a bad past experience, your pain body will be activated. This is called a trigger.

Become aware of what triggers cause any pain body you may have to activate, then take steps to avoid these triggers. The trigger can be a situation, something someone says, feeling a negative emotion, a couple of drinks, or any time when you are not completely present in the moment.

A pain body is like a dark cloud that follows you around everywhere and, although not active all the time, its presence is still often felt. People with large pain bodies carry around a lot of negative emotion that most other people will instinctively want to avoid. Only people with similarly hungry pain bodies will stick around. Having these pain bodies will make you more reactive, distort your thinking, disrupt your relationships, and bring more unhappiness into your world.

Pain bodies are very closely linked with the ego: they both need each other to survive. The ego will look to create enemies and cause drama in that person's life so the pain body can continue to feed. Certain people will react to certain events—not being able to separate their inner unhappiness from the event itself. To others the event will seem trivial, but because the person with the pain body is unaware of their troubled inner state, they blame the event for making them feel that way.

The routine pick-up methods teach that learning the perfect lines and copying someone else's mannerisms can cover up a pain body. However, the student might be smiling and running pick-up "material," but you don't need to be that perceptive to notice that there is a huge ball of unhappy emotions underneath the surface. This ball of unhappy emotion, or pain body, is always looking for the next thing to be unhappy about. It will never get enough.

Unfortunately, students with low levels of self-esteem don't think they are attractive and so in turn are drawn toward learning pick-up lines. This often leads to frustration, an increase in ego, or giving up and declaring that learning "game" doesn't work. Alternatively, they become social robots, living in constant fear that someone will uncover their unhappy selves.

Some people with negative pain bodies will try to be proactive and get things done. This is a good thing but they will be hampered by all the negative emotions that they carry around with them. Invariably they'll make enemies, cause drama, and find reasons for things to go wrong, which will feed their pain bodies.

Some men enter the seduction community because of a lack of love and attention from their mothers. The mother's withdrawal of love creates deep-rooted pain bodies—the son longing for her love, and at the same time resenting her for not giving it to him. Now an adult, every woman he comes into contact with will trigger that pain body, leading to a need to conquer and seduce all women. As soon as a relationship turns intimate or loving, though, the pain body can sabotage this, due to the pent-up anger he has toward his mother.

Having this sort of pain body isn't necessarily a bad thing when starting out, because it will give the man motivation to keep approaching women. After a time, though, this probably isn't the healthiest way in which to live. The pain body should be identified and removed.

HOW TO REMOVE A PAIN BODY

You can break free and remove a pain body instantly; it doesn't have to be a long, drawn-out process. Depending on the strength and size of the pain body, an hour to a few weeks is usually all it takes.

The way to remove a pain body is to do two things:

1. Remove your identification with the pain body. When you can feel the pain body being activated, just say to yourself, "This is a pain body I'm feeling and has no relation to who I am." Become aware of the pain body and let your conscious notice it, the pain body hopes never to be discovered. The old negative emotion may still be present for a few weeks but it will gradually fade away.

2. Don't allow the pain body to become a problem or something that is wrong with you; the ego will love that. Instead, just accept that whatever you are feeling at the moment will pass. At the time a pain body can feel very real and this can lead to tremendous pain. This pain will never kill you but can lead your mind to do things you later regret. It is a product of your past and will disappear forever once you become conscious of it.

REMOVING A PAIN BODY: AN EXAMPLE

Let's say that you break up with a girlfriend and you can't stand the feeling of her being with someone else. This thought might activate a pain body, which leads to anger, jealousy, and other negative emotions. The density of this pain body will determine how badly it affects you. This is purely an ego reaction. Just accept that it is a pain body you are feeling and that it will pass. Remember too, that nothing changes who you are as a person and your experiences.

Before experiencing the pain that is caused by pain bodies it is useful to write down a list of positive reasons for implementing the new change in your life, while you have a clear mind. For example, write a list of reasons why getting back with your ex is a bad thing to do. Then write down a list of all the reasons why being single will be good for you in the long run. This may sound like an uncaring thing to do. I'm not saying you should end up hating your ex; in fact, you should end up wanting her to be happy. For the moment, though, to prevent yourself from doing anything stupid, realigning your beliefs will help you to logically accept the situation.

The ego will probably try to prevent you from writing negative things about your ex. It won't want the pain body to die. Ignore these thoughts, it is just a trick of the mind. As Tolle says in *The Power of Now*, "Nothing can defeat the power of the present moment."

EVERYTHING COUNTS

To become an attractive man, everything counts. You can be really good-looking, which will score you some replication and social value points. However, if you are not confident your overall attractiveness will decrease. It is always a good exercise to take a look at where you are every few months. If you are lacking in a certain area, then take action to improve it.

Being attractive can be described as a bar chart of monthly progress with an attractiveness threshold line at the top. Everything counts in making you a more attractive man. Learning pick-up skills, confidence, humor, positivity, good clothes, working out, a tan, e.t.c., this all counts! When you reach a level of attractiveness that passes the overall threshold, most women will find you sexually attractive. Before reaching a level of overall attractiveness, results will be more hit and miss. The results will probably depend more on fluctuating confidence levels and the situational environment. When you reach and pass the attractiveness threshold you will reach true abundance and consistency with your approaches.

EXERCISE: MY VITAL STATS DASH EXERCISE

This exercise focuses on your attractiveness in a cold-approach situation. If you are looking to transition into a relationship, then ambition and social value will play a lot larger roles. Take some time to fill out the table on the next page, scoring yourself from 1-20, 1-10, and 1-5, the lowest score being "I'm rock bottom in this area" and the highest score being "I could not be any better in this area." Be honest in your assessments, and add up your total score. Highlight just one attribute that you are going to improve over the next couple of weeks. It is always best to focus on one at a time.

ATTRIBUTE	MAX. POINTS	YOUR CURRENT
Confidence	20	
Humor	20	
Positivity	20	
Social value	20	
Dominance	10	
Calmness	10	
Social calibration	10	
Rapport-building	10	
Female friends	10	
Escalation	10	
Fashion	5	
Aesthetics	5	
Intelligence	5	
Ambition	5	
Cheekiness	5	
Male friends	5	
Total	170	

Chapter 7:
Green Vegan Pick-Up Machine

I was on the fence about including some of this information because it borders on being diet information. That said, it is so vitally important in getting a strong inner game that I had no choice. As Bruce Lee said, "Try everything, keep what works, and discard what doesn't." But at least try for a couple of months and observe the changes in yourself and your game. I don't judge anyone for anything, including what they eat, but I do recommend you give it a go.

During my early years of learning success with women I used to drink lots of caffeine such as coffee and energy drinks when I was out. I'd experience massive mood swings and my energy levels were either much too high or much too low. I was unable to get a kiss or extract women because my state was always too erratic.

One of the biggest corner-stones to pick-up is making sure that your confidence is taken care of. When your confidence is good, then it makes it a lot easier for you to calibrate and tweak your verbal game. If a woman rejected your approach but you felt confident and relaxed, then you know it was either because your approach technique was wrong or she was just in a bad mood. If your confidence is weak, then there could be many reasons why she rejected the approach. The two best ways to improve your confidence are through meditation and the food that you eat.

Eating the correct foods makes a massive difference to how you feel about yourself. Starch and meat used to be slave food. Look at the evolution and awareness of the typical person sitting in McDonalds, Burger King, KFC, or a fast food restaurant of your choice. Go in there and take a look around. Do they mostly look healthy or unhealthy? Do they appear to have high or low self-esteem? Are they beautiful or ugly? Are they calm or angry? Now take a trip to your local organic food store and have a look at the typical people in there. You will be amazed at the difference.

Cool, confident people eat natural, healthy food. Most celebrities will eat very healthy balanced diets. They might appear on McDonalds or Coca Cola adverts but they probably are going to go home and eat a healthy salad. Look up celebrity vegetarians or vegans on Google; you will be amazed about how many famous people there are.

Part of being a pick-up artist is learning to see the matrix and removing attachment from social conditioning.

FOR HEALTH

For health the simple message is: living foods give life and dead foods create death. Living foods are foods that are still alive and raw and have electricity in them. Just like us, vegetables and fruits are made up of cells, which can either be dead or alive. If you eat fresh food in its raw state, then the cells will still be alive. When you eat raw food you are taking a living energy into your body. In cooked food the cells have already been destroyed and the food is dead. Dead food takes more cellular energy to break down than it will give you in return.

Living foods are vitally important for pick-up because of the law of state transfer (see pages 145–149). How you feel the woman will feel. You want to be approaching women full of energy and life, and overflowing with positivity and happiness. A lot of students have seen me approach the same women as them and get much better reactions. State transfer is what is happening here; this is my secret. The way I cultivate my good state is by making sure that I eat the living, water-rich foods.

Eat fruit for energy and vegetables for healing and calming the nervous system. The simple sugars that are found in fruit are vital for our cells to function optimally. Fruit sugar gives us dynamic cellular energy full of living vibration. This is what you want. White sugar is bad because it is manmade and our bodies have trouble processing and utilizing it.

Caffeine and white sugar will give you stimulated energy. In other words they are irritants to the body. Stimulated energy always has an up and a down. Dynamic fruit energy, or simple sugars, will never give you a down; they provide a stable high. It becomes almost impossible to manage state control and inner game while on a stimulated energy high. The body is not at peace, in fact it is in an erratic state of stimulation. The up and down mood swings are exactly the reactive type of behavior you want to avoid. The woman should be the emotional one, not you.

DETOX

I'm certainly no doctor and I wouldn't suggest giving anyone medical advice but I do believe that taking a more healthy approach to eating will lead to you being happier and more confident. As with any detox plan, it's always a good idea to check with your doctor, particularly if you have any medical conditions.

Detox is about understanding that the body is the healer and that energy is at the core of healing. When you eat only living, easily digestible foods, then your body will start to have extra energy. All the energy that was previously spent digesting cooked foods will be used on fixing old problems which had been previously pushed to one side. Over time toxins accumulate in the body, so when you start eating raw foods your body begins a process of detoxification The body will start to eliminate toxins and heal damaged cells. Apart from the obvious health benefits there are other things to consider for the pick-up artist: clear skin, good energy, a clear mind, and, perhaps most importantly, a calming of the nervous system. When exposed to high levels of stimulating, hormonal foods our nervous systems get over anxious and confused. When you detox, your body will start to fix this and you will begin to feel calmer when approaching women. Which is more attractive, approaching a woman nervous or approaching her calmly?

Try to eat only fruit during the day and then a jumbo-size salad at night. Eat as much fruit and salad as you want; there is no restriction or calorie counting for this. You will lose weight, as it is impossible to put on weight while on a raw-food detox. Make sure you don't have any cooked or processed food in the salad—just raw, uncooked vegetables. Try doing this for five days straight. Notice the difference in how you feel from eating cooked food to eating raw food. The difference is like night and day.

You might start to experience a healing crisis as you approach the end of the five days. This is when the detox is actually taking place. Because fruits are so alive and easily digestible, the body will have lots of excess energy and so will use it and start to repair itself. You might notice mild cold or flu-type symptoms. These are actually good because these are signs that the body is getting rid of toxicity and healing itself.

During this time you might notice that emotions well up, particularly from childhood. Emotions stick to cells, so when you are detoxing, both your cells and the emotions stuck to them will be detoxed too. Be aware of what is happening, don't place any meaning on it, and keep moving forward. Let these emotions out and they won't come back and continue to hold you back.

During my first detox, which lasted ten days, I felt myself getting very frustrated and angry for no reason. These emotions had obviously been stored from childhood. At the end of the detox I felt at peace, like a massive weight had been lifted from my shoulders.

WHAT TO EAT BEFORE YOU GO SARGING

Before you go out it is important to eat lots of natural carbohydrates. The fruits with the most carbohydrates are bananas and dates. Try mixing the two of them in a blender with some spinach and coconut water. I will often have this before I go out. It gives me energy, hydrates me, and the spinach will ground me. Boom, I'm ready to rock.

Celery is also fantastic because it is very alkaline, cheap, and calms the nervous system. So, if you are getting social anxiety, I'd drink celery and apple juice like it was going out of style. Lettuce is another key part of my diet. Lettuce is a sedative; it calms the body and can help you relax and sleep. Don't worry, you aren't going to fall asleep on the dance floor, but you will notice a greater feeling of peace. This is how you want to be approaching women; feeling relaxed, calm, and at peace.

For more recipes visit the blog www.puamethod.com/wordpress/.

WHY TO CONSIDER TRYING MEAT ALTERNATIVES

There are lots of health reasons why reducing or giving up your meat intake is beneficial. It will cut down the risk of heart disease, cancer, high cholesterol, osteoporosis, and arthritis. Also by stopping eating meat you reduce the load on the planet. This subject is outside the scope of this book but if you are interested I highly recommend reading *The Kind Diet* by Alicia Silverstone.

THE MAIN BENEFITS TO DROPPING OR REDUCING YOUR INTAKE OF MEAT

Meat is hard to digest: All the carnivores in the animal kingdom have very short intestinal tracts. Also, they have a lie-down or a nap after eating each meal. Meat is very hard for the body to process, so all the body's energy goes into trying to digest it. How do you feel after a large steak? Tired. What about after eating fruit? It is almost impossible to sit still.

This stuff might seem inconsequential, but every weekend on boot camp there are students who eat burgers and fries. They then experience a massive drop in energy and performance for the evening session. Fruit is digested quickly and will give you instant energy.

Meat is full of antibiotics: Animals raised in confined, dirty, stressful environments tend to get sick and are given antibiotics as a preventive measure. Seventy percent of all antibiotics sold in the USA go to livestock. These antibiotics are then passed to you when you eat meat. These will wipe out your own healthy intestinal bacteria, making you more susceptible to illness and disease.

Meat is full of hormones: Cattle, chickens, and pigs are routinely pumped full of hormones to increase their muscle mass and size. Eggs and farmed fish are also packed full of hormones. These hormones, when digested, have a direct effect on how you feel. Your body doesn't need extra hormones and so these will take you out of balance and away from an ideal feeling of peace.

MORE ABOUT MEAT

Some people report that they gain energy from eating meat. The energy they think they are feeling is actually the dead animals' adrenalin that was caused by the slaughter process. This energy at the very least is passive aggressive and not the dynamic happy energy that is so powerful for meeting women.

The animal slaughter process is not a calming one. Cows have a bolt gun fired at their head; in over 40 percent of cases this does not kill them. They are then hung up, still alive, and have their throats slit. We don't like blood in our meat so the cow has to be drained. Then the cow will be skinned, even if it is still alive, and in many cases the cow will still be kicking for freedom as their legs are cut off.

This slaughter process is the same with all edible animals. We are led to believe that the animals live happy lives, roaming green meadows to a ripe old age until they have to be put down. This is not the case; most of these animals never see the light of day.

That being the case, the adrenalin, stress, and hormones coursing through the animals' veins when being led to slaughter ends up in you. Is it any wonder why a lot of us feel stressed, anxious, or nervous? To attract women to you it is important that you are thriving and not just surviving.

Generally, as a species, we are getting weaker—heart disease, cancer, weak eyes, balding, and beauty issues. I have a medium constitution. I noticed my overall health deteriorating from the age of about 24. That said, because I was raised on white sugar, meat, and dairy I was always socially anxious and erratic. Some of you may be able to get away with making bad food choices and still be calm and happy. This is probably down to genes. The vast majority of us can't and if you want to really get your dating life handled, then you should test out a vegan diet. Do it for a couple of months and see how it works out for you.

BUILD MUSCLE WITHOUT MEAT

There are times when I like to detox and times when I like to put on mass. A lot of people think that when we eat meat we are ripping muscle from the animal and putting it directly on our own. Unfortunately, it doesn't work like that. The body breaks down all food that you eat in order to extract the useful parts. When you lift weights you tear the muscle and, in order to repair the tear, the body uses amino acids which are broken-down protein.

The key to muscle-building is to get a wide variety of amino acids from the food you eat and lift heavy weights. You can get amino acids from a variety of healthy natural foods—spinach, kale, rice, nuts, and seeds are a few of my favorites. There are hundreds of vegan professional bodybuilders and athletes out there from all over the world who choose a healthy raw lifestyle for performance reasons only. For more detailed information on this, please visit www.puamethod.com/wordpress/bodybuildingpua/.

CONSIDER TRYING DAIRY ALTERNATIVES

I can hear you saying, "Milk is bad for us too? No way, I used to drink milk all the time at school. Where else do we get our calcium from?" Right? I hear you. I was raised on dairy too because it was meant to be good for the bones.

Calcium is an abundant mineral; you can find it in all fruit and vegetables, with the highest concentration found in sesame seeds. Calcium needs magnesium to be properly utilized by the body and there is four times the amount of calcium to magnesium in cows' milk. We actually utilize more calcium from fruit juice than we do from milk.

Breast milk is OK to drink up until the age of two, but after that the benefits to the growing child are limited. Unless it is for some kinky sex game; in which case, as long as no one gets hurt, or goes hungry, I won't hold it against you.

Human enzyme production for handling milk is much lower than the a cow's. Most children lose their dairy enzymes altogether at the ages of three or four because breastfeeding would have stopped long before then. Are you lactose intolerant? Most people are and don't even realize it.

With humans not having the proper enzymes to process cows' milk, we suffer with digestive problems and mucus congestion. Colds, flu, and any lymphatic issue are mostly due to dairy products. One of my instructors recently started drinking milk for muscle-building. Within a week or two all his childhood acne had come back.

Skin conditions are all linked to blockages of the lymphatic system. You have two fluids in your body: blood distributes nutrients and the lymphatic fluid removes waste. Dairy is highly mucus-forming and is the biggest reason why the lymphatic system gets blocked.

So, if you want great skin and high energy, you must cut dairy out of your diet. There are lots of alternative delicious, non-dairy foods. For a more detailed look please visit www.puamethod.com/wordpress/dairypua/.

MASSAGE

There is nothing better than getting a massage before you go out to talk to women. It gets all the stress out of your shoulders, or wherever it accumulates for you. A massage will get you talking and used to female attention. Also, it is really nice to feel human touch, especially if you haven't for a while.

Many massage therapists can be booked to come to your house and massage you in your home. My recommendation is that you try different masseuses until you find one that you like. I'd try the most attractive women first, for obvious reasons. Also, it is a great way to get used to being around attractive women. The game is not different for hot women but learning to feel comfortable around them can be, and that only comes with experience and exposure.

Get a massage once or twice per month and learn to relax and let go. When the woman is there try not to practice game on her and instead just be yourself. It is important to give yourself as many reference points as possible that you are enough as you are. So being yourself with a woman is one of the first steps to training your brain to realize that you can share a great experience with her without needing to be anyone you are not.

COLONICS

A colonic is a cleansing process where warm water is passed through the colon. It is a gentle procedure that can have aggressive results as it can break loose plaque that has been fixed on the colon wall for years.

They aren't cheap and they can be a little uncomfortable. That said they are a fantastic way of helping you to truly let go. It depends on how healthy and how old you are as to how much fecal matter you will have impacted on your intestinal wall.

Colonics aid relief of acidosis, back pain, headaches, and fevers. The major benefit is gaining a clear head and feeling a lot calmer. Also, training yourself to let go and surrender to the moment is important to pick-up.

HAIR LOSS

Research indicates that over two-thirds of men in the UK will experience a degree of hair loss before they reach the age of 35. So, although I'd love to have a Christian Bale-type hairline, I must accept that it is a very common problem.

Many guys worry about going bald and actively look to settle down as soon as this happens. Who do you think is going to have more power in that relationship, or divorce the other, a few years down the line?

Hair loss really isn't as big of a deal as you might imagine. With younger women it might be a bit more of a problem as you will be in the minority compared to the men her age. These women will also have less social experience, and so rely on what social conditioning teaches them that they should be attracted to. They date the stereotypical guys for a few years but often realize, depending on the guy, that they are inexperienced, act childish, are lazy, passive, or negative, and don't meet a woman's emotional needs, and then leave them.

Your behavior and social experience is a lot more important than anything about your personal appearance. Women want to feel the emotions that they think a good-looking guy will give them—the feelings of being weak at the knees, shy, submissive, and in love. Younger women might find it more of an issue if a man is bald but they soon realize that good-looking doesn't always equal attraction.

Get a stylist. Cool clothes, piercings, and tattoos (fake or real) can really help you stand out, too. Make sure your smile is white and your teeth are fixed—you want to be a happy smiling person.

If you are going through hair loss, be aware of your value. If you are dressed generically, you have no women with you, and you aren't feeling confident, then being good-looking can help in your favor. If you aren't really good-looking, then make the best of what you have got. Standing out with a fake tattoo or piercing, approaching confidently and dominantly, making her laugh, building a connection—this is so far removed and so much cooler than what other guys are doing. I assure you, hair is a non-issue.

Another realization I've had is that if my state and game are just a little better than a good-looking guy with a full head of hair, I will get all the attention. Obviously there are exceptions to this, especially where the guy is the woman's perfect type. In most cases, though, I will provoke much greater attraction and the choice to see the woman again. This level of entitlement comes down to knowing what you are doing. I believe I am one of the best-looking guys around. Delusional? Maybe. Effective? A big fat yes.

Final proof, if you need it, is that there is always a subset of women who like every characteristic that you have. I once knew a woman who just loved the tennis player Andre Agassi and that whole bald bad-boy look in general. There are also women that love bodybuilder types, red heads, tennis players, and men with beards. You name it, there is a subset of women who just love it. The important thing is to stand out rather than to blend in and to be confident about demonstrating who you are.

The Action

(Yang)

Chapter 8:
Approach Anxiety

Approach Anxiety (AA) is a fear that arises when approaching a woman or a group of people. This fear stems partly from a hard-wired response that has evolved from tribal caveman days: in tribal times, if you approached a woman who belonged to the tribal leader he could kill you. Or, if you approached a woman and your interest wasn't reciprocated, then she would tell the rest of the women in the tribe that you were not worthy and this would mean that your genes would not get passed on. Approach Anxiety can also stem from bad experiences, low self-esteem, poor diet, having your mind too focused on the future, negativity, and having a small comfort zone, meaning you aren't used to new experiences like talking to strangers. If you don't suffer from Approach Anxiety and can approach with few problems, then I recommend you skip this chapter. Reading it will only make you think that talking to women is a big deal, when really it is not.

I CAN RELATE

For those who do have an intermediate or strong level of AA, I can sympathize and relate to what you're feeling. You see a woman that you want to talk to, but something stops you. I used to worry a great deal about approaching women. There are many different levels of shared loss, from a mild indifference to a strong physical reaction.

Growing up in a village, it never seemed socially acceptable for me to approach women I didn't know. There was also the risk of it going badly and that the woman might be friends with people that I was friends with and tell them I wasn't cool. When I moved to the city I still carried those same limiting beliefs—people are busy, don't waste their time, women don't want to be approached, I have nothing interesting to say. These limiting beliefs produced stress in me many times and held me back from approaching women altogether.

CHANGE YOUR STATE OF MIND

We have lots of different states of mind: sociable, logical, caring, analytical, aggressive, talkative, fun. Sometimes you will see a woman that you want to talk to, but you aren't in a sociable frame of mind. I used to work as a Java programmer. For those who aren't in the geek gang, Java is a computer language for making applications— usually web-based. I found that on my lunch break or after work I'd never feel like being sociable. This would frustrate me. I'd notice a woman I liked, but all I could think about was how to cast integers into doubles and other Java classes. I suspected that these subjects would not get her juices flowing or lead to cuddles later on in the night.

At this time I mostly went out with my old school friends, because what I noticed about the guys from work was that they never had much fun. I don't say this in a mean way—I still liked them as people—but there was never any joking around or playful banter. It was mostly logical conversations about computer processors and how one operating system is better than another.

Some of the best states of mind to be in when you are meeting women are: talkative, confident, playful, dominant, cheeky, positive, happy. Having said that, if you are in a bad state of mind, just accept it and don't get frustrated. Getting annoyed that you're out of state will just create more barriers. If you are sad, unhappy, or depressed, accept that state. "Maybe I am feeling sad, that's cool." This acceptance will improve your chances of shifting into a better state.

BABY STEPS TO TAKING THE RIGHT ACTION

Sometimes you can find yourself in a really bad state and feel that it's almost impossible to approach. In this situation you need to start small. Below is a six-step exercise that I sometimes use to get warmed up. Do these exercises all on the same day. Some of the exercises you may find challenging, so I recommend for the first couple of times that you take a friend or wingman and do them together. Spend no longer than two hours doing the exercises in order on any one day.

1. Ask for the time

Approach three women or three groups of women and ask them for the time. When they give you the time, say thank you and leave. Do not continue to game them after they give you the time; this is important.

2. Ask for directions

Ask three women or three groups of women for directions to either the rail station or post office. Listen to the directions and then say thank you and leave. It is important not to continue gaming them after you get the directions.

3. Ask for the time while wearing a watch or holding your phone in your hand

Ask three women or three groups of women for the time. When they tell you the time, say thank you and leave. If they ask you why you haven't looked at your own watch or phone, simply tell them that you think it might be broken.

4. Ask three couples the time

Approach three couples and ask each woman for the time. Don't look at the man, only look at the woman when you are asking for the time. When he or she gives you the time, thank them and leave.

5. Ask for the time without eye contact

Approach three women or three groups of women and ask them for the time without making eye contact. Either look at the floor or look past them. Be strict with yourself, no cheating, make no eye contact. When they tell you the time, say thank you and leave. This will feel weird but there is a reason for and order to each of these exercises.

6. Ask whether they'd like to go for a coffee

Approach three women or three groups of women and ask them if they'd like to go for a coffee with you: "I know this is going to sound really random, but would you like to go for a coffee with me?" If she says "yes", then you must politely decline. If she asks for your phone number, then you can't give it to her. Also you can't ask or take her phone number either, even if she is your dream woman and is saying yes.

Congratulations on completing the exercise. If you repeat these steps a few times you will notice that your AA will disappear.

If you didn't complete all of the steps, go back to Step 1 and start again. You must complete all of the steps in order.

If you are struggling with one particular step, take a friend out with you when you are doing it. It will help to cheer each other on. Also, you can give your friend some money. Tell him that for every approach that you do he has to give you back a certain amount of the money. Give your friend an amount of money that is going to motivate you.

Combine the information in this chapter with that in the section on momentum (see pages 124–128) for optimum results. You need to aggressively challenge your AA day after day, repeating these steps, until it has disappeared.

If you are still having problems with AA and you can't even bring yourself to commit to Step 1 of the exercise, then I recommend one-to-one training rather than boot camp. Make it clear when booking through PUA Method that you suffer from anxiety. Visualization techniques, belief rewiring, and inner-game tweaking will be carried out to remove that anxiety.

Chapter 9: Momentum

"A journey of a thousand miles begins with a single step." – Tao Te Ching

Being good at pick-up is a skill set that you can learn just like anything else. You need to learn the techniques and then practice them over and over again, the same way as you would if you were learning to play a new sport. The more that you practice in an intelligent way, the more you will see your results with women improve. It is not realistic for me to expect that my level of pick-up skill will be the same if I spend long hours working in the office compared to being out and socializing on the street. It just doesn't work like that.

Take tennis, do you think Rafael Nadal can just walk on to the Wimbledon Center Court and his game is immediately at the top level? Nadal practices virtually every day and warms up before every match that he plays.

I'm not saying you need to dedicate your life to getting good with women, but you do need to practice regularly.

COMMIT TO PICK-UP

The more time you spend talking to women, the better you will become at it. It is nothing to do with looks or money but literally how much you want to succeed. Are you going to be the guy who actually gets a great skill set with women and gets this part of his life handled? Or will you be the dabbler who tries a few things, gives up as soon as it gets a little tricky, and then goes on Internet forums to blame everyone but himself for his lack of success? You must be going out at least three to six times per week, once or twice is not enough. What is more important, the latest computer game or getting your dating life sorted?

To live the pick-up lifestyle you must commit fully to it until you find a woman that keeps your interest. You can't dip your toe into the water occasionally; you must dive in and fully commit to stay there until you reach your goal. Is it healthy to be going out five times a week for years approaching women? Probably not. I'd imagine your goals will start to shift once you get pick-up handled.

For you to get to a level where you feel like you can go out and in a month or two you can find a beautiful, high-self-esteem woman to be your girlfriend can take time. Some guys can get to that level really quickly. For other guys it might take one, two, or even three years of hard work to get there. Regardless of how long it takes, I don't think it really matters because the journey is the fun part. When I was first going out learning pick-up it was really fun despite being rejected all of the time. When I got really good at pick-up, it was fun too, but for different reasons. Did it become more fun? For a few months, maybe, and then it was just the same level of fun. I got into a relationship and that's also fun, but again for different reasons. So, wherever you're at, it's always fun.

The important thing is that you commit to the journey and you stay on it, however long it takes you. It could be that you take three years to get really good at pick-up, but your friend takes just a weekend. Myself and PUA Method instructor Roj both started pick-up at the same time. He got really good after doing one boot camp, 23 numbers in a week, and was dating hot women shortly after. Me? I took longer, probably four years of trying to figure it all out for myself (I never took a boot camp). Even now I look at Roj and there are things that he still does much better than me. However, there are now things that I can do much better than him and the time it took me to learn these things means I have a more solid understanding of how to break social interactions down.

If I had got good at pick-up really quickly, then perhaps I wouldn't even be writing this book right now. Perhaps taking longer to learn pick-up will enable you to become really proficient in business meetings, or become the leader of a social group. These are just suggestions, but my point is that you never know the reason for things. Often things that seemed frustrating or negative at the time turned out to be some of the greatest gifts I could have received when I look back on them now. Just trust that it will all work out for a good reason in the end.

CONSISTENCY IS KEY

By going out consistently you will start to build up momentum. This means that eventually you will start to get success and that success will improve your beliefs about yourself with women, and that increase in your confidence will get you more success. This success cycle will continue to strengthen and grow as long as you keep going out and approaching in an intelligent way.

It is best to approach as many beautiful women as you can. The streets or higher-end venues are fantastic for this. When you finally get used to talking to beautiful women, you will experience a feeling of "letting go" and relax around them. When you feel relaxed around women, they will feel relaxed around you. This letting go will open up a door of feminine opportunities for you. As you start to reach higher and higher levels of momentum you will rapidly build new reference points of what you can achieve. New beliefs will form inside you that you can date the type of women that you desire.

IMPLEMENTING A HABIT

So, you resolve to get this thing with women sorted once and for all. You commit to going out a certain number of times per week to talk to strangers. It's all going great, you're happy, and progress is being made. You even tell your friends about your new habit and the success you are having. Then you backslide and stop going out. What went wrong? Why would we do this? Is it because we are lazy or that we don't care? Not necessarily. Going back to old behaviors is a natural mechanism that we all have. It is called homeostasis.

MAKING THE CHANGE

Your body is only interested in staying alive, so as soon as something changes your natural equilibrium, your body instinctively looks to right this. This natural balancing is called homeostasis. Your body doesn't realize that becoming more social is actually going to benefit you. Instead, the only thing it recognizes is that extra effort is being used and this might threaten your survival, so it shuts down. This happens a lot during boot camps when a student is being pushed far outside of his comfort zone. He will start to feel tired and sometimes even physically sick. This intense reaction is dealt with by acknowledging homeostasis and resuming the training. Learning pick-up might feel a bit uncomfortable at first but accepting this discomfort will enable you to see your results with women improve.

So how does homeostasis affect us when we are implementing a new habit of becoming more social? Well, your brain will come up with a million reasons why approaching women is stupid—it's too hard, it's creepy, you don't need to bother. These all come from within the context of "My life is fine as it is."

I recommend that you write down all the reasons why going out and regularly approaching women will benefit you. I do this every time I want to implement a new habit in my life, whatever it is. I then take this list and pin it to my bedroom wall. This gives your brain evidence to stay on track with your new practice, even when you start to resist it or you don't feel like practicing that day.

THOSE AROUND YOU

Homeostasis can also occur with your friends and family. For example, learning social skills and developing your confidence might not be something that your friends and family want to see. Despite wishing you well, it is possible that they will try to hold you back. Change can be scary. Those close to you may think that you won't like them anymore when you change. They might say things like "Just be yourself" or "Learning that is weird." Respect their opinion but push on anyway, making sure not to rub your progress in their face.

THIRTY DAYS OF IMPLEMENTATION

Typically, to implement a new habit you will need to keep it up for thirty days. Usually a basic pattern of enthusiasm, turning to resentment, ripening to integration will occur. Whether it's going for a run every day or talking to a stranger, implementing either follows a similar pattern. Becoming aware of this pattern is half the battle, the other half is determination and giving yourself a compelling reason to keep the habit up.

Chapter 10:
PUA Method Interaction

It is important not to have a strict structure when dealing with social interactions. A rigid structure only offers the student a different cage to the one he was in previously. It is useful, however, to have a basic idea of what to say in an interaction. Naturals get this through noticing patterns of success in the thousands of social interactions that they have. Let's speed up this process, though, by outlining the basic structure that you should be working with.

NON-LINEAR STRUCTURE—V - O - A - Q - C - S

V = social value. Peacocking, proof of social skills, demonstrations of social alliances. Social value means that you carry an obvious level of attractiveness into the opener phase. This social value will be visible to people around you. There is no point having high value that no one knows about. Social value is not as important as being an attractive person, but having social value can mean women give you more of a chance.

O = opener. Can be anything to start a conversation. The opener is how you start a conversation with a woman or group of people.

A = attraction. Teasing, role-playing, stories, humor. An attractive man will demonstrate the qualities of an alpha male. The top three characteristics of an alpha male are confidence, humor, and positivity.

Q = qualification. Having boundaries and standards. The qualification phase is about you demonstrating that you aren't a pushover. A strong man will try to find things out about new women before being completely won over by them. Qualification is also a demonstration of personal boundaries, such as dealing with bad behavior or putting troublemakers in their place.

C = comfort: commonalities, venue changing, cold reading. The comfort phase is where you get to know a woman on a deeper level. You want to feel connected to each other and get her to open up about her life. This can be done through conversation and also through techniques. These techniques will be explained in greater detail on pages 141–143.

S = sexual. Slow talk, looking at lips, touch, kiss. The sexual phase is where you take the interaction to a more seductive tone. This can be done with words or by using body language.

This structure is non-linear, which means that you can do pretty much anything at any stage of the interaction. However, it is useful to remember that sometimes "attraction" comes before "qualification" and that comes before "comfort." There are always anomalies; for example, the woman could just be in a sexual mood and so communicates to you through touch. In this case, you can start with "attraction" and move on to "sexual," avoiding "comfort" and "qualification" altogether. Above all, let your social intuition guide you, bearing in mind that you will have to mess up many times so you can learn. Practice makes perfect.

INDIRECT OPENER

An indirect opener is used to start a conversation that does not reveal your intentions or show specific interest. A good indirect opener will engage the woman in a topic of conversation that she will feel compelled to talk about. Relationships, some kind of drama, fashion, and seeking out female advice are all good topics of conversation.

Indirect openers are useful for a shy woman or if the woman is not in a talkative state. Opening in this way will allow her to become talkative. You are taking the pressure off two strangers meeting for the first time by starting an interesting conversation. Here are a few indirect openers to get you started:

- "Hi, I'm looking for a good book on fashion and I think you might be able to help me."

- "Hi, I'm new to here, what are the best bars/restaurants/places to go around here?"

- "Hi, I'm looking for a cool present for my friend Gemma, can you recommend something?"

"Hey, what is the occasion?"

"Hey, who has the best outfit on tonight?"

Don't stare at the woman first. Women are very aware when men stare at them and they will put their defences up. If you do become aware that a woman is close by, use your peripheral vision to check she is attractive to you. Then open straight away with no hesitation or delay. Go for what you want. It is best to look natural and authentic even when going indirect. If you are looking at books in a bookshop ask her, "What's the best book you have read on fashion/art/culture?" If she is holding an apple, turn to her and ask, "Is that as tasty as it looks?" You could even point to yourself when you say the word tasty—this is known as a neuro linguistic pattern (NLP) technique—the idea is to make her think that you are tasty. Point to yourself when saying words like "desire," "attraction," "tasty," "excitement" and she will feel those emotions toward you. This is not required, but occasional use of this technique can be a very powerful way of creating attraction in her.

Use your environment and stay in the moment. It is important not to think "what could impress her." Instead, come from a place of curiosity and fun. The main advantage of indirect opening is that it will feel romantic to the woman, like it was meant to be. With direct opening it creates a lot of attraction in the woman but after the interaction she might feel that you say the same thing to every woman you meet. With direct opening you need to spend more time in the qualifying and comfort phases; with indirect you don't need to spend as much time in these phases. If you can't see anything in the environment to be curious about, then use one of the recommended openers above.

It is always good to have a couple of openers memorized in case you can't think of anything to say. I never want to be in a situation where I don't open because I can't think of something cool to say. I just open anyway because she could be my dream woman. Finally, if you feel nervous before you approach, then tell her, "Hi, I'm a bit nervous to ask you but can you recommend a good book on fashion?" There is no point trying to cover up feelings of nervousness by pretending to be confident. It will just come off as fake and inauthentic.

You want to always be real because it is a lot more attractive to be genuinely nervous than to be nervous and faking confidence. Being real demonstrates high value because you aren't selling yourself out by trying to impress her and you end up accepting yourself. Also, by accepting this feeling, it is going to disappear a lot more quickly and you will start to feel confident again. If you resist the emotion and pretend it is not there, then it will continue to stay in your body because it is trapped. This will work with any negative emotion: anxiety, nervousness, shyness, or fear. Feel it, accept it, communicate it, and it will go. Remember: what you resist will persist.

The next approach you make, you will feel a lot more confident: by accepting your negative emotions you can become authentically confident. I have successfully picked up beautiful women while feeling sad, angry, or stressed and communicated this to them like this: "Hi, I'm feeling angry and I'm buying a present for my friend Gemma. Can you recommend something?" A bit of angry chit chat and I start to feel better and before I know it I've got her number and we're going on a date the following week. This happens all the time because it is impossible to always be in a good mood. We are only human, and so are women and they will understand about showing your real emotions.

DIRECT OPENER

Direct opening is a lot of fun. It's high risk, but it's the most rewarding way of opening available. This type of opening shows a lot of confidence and rarely happens during the day as most men feel more comfortable approaching women in the evening. With direct opening, you notice something that you like about the woman and then confidently and positively you stop her and tell her. "Hey, I love your style and had to come over and say hi. My name is Rob."

Once you have given your reason for approaching her, there's no need to keep the opener going or look for an elaborate transition; you can just go straight to humor and qualification (see pages 155–164). So, for example, mention that you love her style and then move to another topic of conversation. Don't follow up with "Where did you get your shoes from?" or "What make is that purse?" It's obvious you aren't a fashion consultant, so don't pretend to be. If she looks a little awkward, apologize for startling her and explain that it's completely random but you had to come over and say hi.

There is a lot of debate as to whether you have to be good-looking for a direct opener to work. I used to be good-looking, a 9.8 on the hot-or-not scale, thank you very much. These days I've lost a bit of hair and would probably rate myself as a 7. The point is, if you feel like you are good-looking enough, then it doesn't matter, but if you are thinking "She is far too good for me," then it probably will matter and your approach won't go well. She'll pick up on your lack of confidence in your voice, posture, eye contact, smile, dominance, the way you move, and many other subtle clues. If you walk up to her feeling completely entitled, she will presume there must be some reason that you feel like this. This will give you time to demonstrate attractive qualities and build a connection.

THE DIRECT STREET APPROACH

The direct street approach is very efficient as with this approach there is no need to warm up the room or demonstrate any social values before you open. You literally see a woman you like and run up to her, the action of a free man! You can try this during the day or at night but at night do make sure you are in a busy, well-lit area so as not to alarm her.

The key to this approach is to get your opening technique right. If the women are not stopping for you it is either your state, your appearance, or the technique that you are using is wrong. Your personality has nothing to do with it at this point. Ideally, put yourself in a peaceful or sexual state for approaching (see State Transfer, pages 145–149). If you can't, then second best is to accept however you are feeling at that moment. Make sure you look presentable, a unique fashion style is a bonus but not necessary. Next comes the technique. All rules in pick-up can be broken, but I will give you the most efficient way of opening successfully.

RUN TO HER

Run up to the woman from behind as this makes you less threatening than if you were to run up to her from in front. (How much more pressure are you placing on the woman by running up in front of her?) As you run from behind around to the front of her, look at her as you run round. Do not run or walk in front of her and then spin round and say hi. The motion should be fluid; you saw her and you are now running up to her.

It is crucial that you leave enough room between you and the woman when you run around the front of her, about 5–8 feet (1.5–2.5 meters), depending on how fast the woman is walking. The faster she is walking, the more space you need to leave. She has to hear what you are saying before she has walked past you otherwise she is rarely going to come back and chat. At every boot camp I have to tell students to leave more room; it is a common error but it's easy to correct.

You don't have to smile. It is better to be true to how you are feeling at that moment. Even if you feel sad, it is OK to show this: "Hey, I was having the winter blues today but I saw you and I had to come over and say hi. Your black outfit reminded me of a ninja." She will giggle if it is delivered correctly. It is obviously best to feel happy rather than sad, but equally it is better to accept that you feel sad rather than fake happiness. The woman will be looking at your sub-communications, i.e. your body language, energy, and vocal tonality, to see whether you are genuine or not. I have picked up many, many times while feeling like a soulless troll. This is because I accepted it and was congruent with my troll-like qualities.

As soon as you see a woman that you like, just start running. Don't think "What should I say next?" Just run. This is because you may only have a very short time frame in which to approach her. She might walk into a store or get on a bus. Yes, it is true that you could wait for her to come back out of the store (or whatever the situation may be) and then approach, but it will make you needier by the second. By waiting for her you will be investing in a woman that you know nothing about. This will lead you to wanting the interaction to go well for no reason other than the fact that you've spent time and energy waiting for her. So just run up to her as soon as you see her.

DELIVERING THE OPENER

Next you need to deliver the opener. The best way to do this is along the lines of:

Compliment + unique humor = attraction

Compliment = "I love your style. I had to come over and meet you." +

Unique humor = "You guys reminded me of the Charlie's Angels."

The opener above is an example of what I might deliver to a group of three women. The compliment is standard; it means "You are cute, I love your style, you are sexy." It is OK to open with just that, but to really make the conversation "sticky," which means she wants to stick around, add some unique humor as well.

Here are some examples of openers.

For a group of three women:

"Guys, I love your style, you remind me..... of the Charlie's Angels. I had to come over and meet you."

For a group of four women:

"I love your style. I had to come over and meet you." + "You guys remind me of the film Sex in the City."

For a woman with a brimmed hat:

"Hey, I love your style. I had to come over and meet you." + "Your hat reminds me of Indiana Jones."

For a woman with a hippy or flowery style:

"Hey, I love your style. I had to come over and say hi." + "Your dress makes me imagine you sat round a campfire playing a guitar."

The time to think about what unique humor to use is when you are running. The more you use the direct street approach, the better you will get at thinking of things to say. Maybe try to remember one of the openers that you've learned that could apply to this woman. If you don't manage to think of anything unique by the time you reach her, then just open with the compliment. The compliment is actually a very efficient way to approach; it is just that the unique humor is the cherry on top of the cake.

NORMAL CONVERSATION

As soon as you've delivered the opener and she has stopped, then step across her path round to the other side of her and keep talking. This means she will turn to face you, away from where she was walking and may even forget where she was walking to in the first place. This is a nice psychological technique to increase the chances of the interaction going well. Don't look at your feet while you step to the other side of her; your movements should be fluid.

If she looks like she is about to leave, or in a rush, then give a time constraint, such as: "I can only stay for a minute because I'm meeting my friend Candy for a coffee" or "I can only stay for a minute because I'm on my way to the studio." As soon as the opener has been delivered and a time constraint used you can progress to normal conversation. The attraction part of the pick-up has already been taken care of through your display of confidence in approaching her direct on the street and through your unique humor.

A good technique for normal conversation is to make a statement and then ask a question.

Statement + question = conversation

For example:

"It's my first time in London and I went to see the band Oasis last night. Are you a tourist or do you live here?"

"OMG I went to the Imax cinema to see a horror yesterday, it was fantastic. What type of films are you into?"

"I checked out X club last night, it was really cool. Are you a party girl or are you a stay in and watch a DVD girl?"

Focus on being present and responding to what she says and be willing to ask questions. Go through the other remaining phases: qualification, comfort, and then either get a phone number to close or go on an instant date. It is possible to enter the seduction phase on the street and get a kiss or even go back to yours or her place. This is not common but if she is attracted to you and not in a rush, then you can go for it. For more information on the seduction phase see pages 179–182.

DEMONSTRATE THAT YOU WILL BE HAVING FUN WITH OR WITHOUT HER

It's important to understand that a lot of women will have had many a night ruined because they started talking to a guy and then ended up getting stalked for the rest of the evening. This is why women have a protection shield. Sounds pretty reasonable to me. Give the woman the impression that you aren't that bothered by the interaction and that you can have fun without her. This is called giving a time constraint and it is best to use it when you feel that the woman is about to say she needs to leave. Giving the time constraint will buy you a few minutes with her.

A way to do this is to say:

"Quick question..."

or

"I've only got a minute, but..."

When you become good at pick-up you often don't need to say things like this. You will subliminally communicate that you are a cool guy and that you can have fun with or without her. Getting to this position can take several months of development and practice. It depends on where you're starting from.

ATTRACTION PHASE IN NIGHT GAME

In night game you can do any of the openers listed earlier, so try all of them, and see which ones suit you best. Once you have opened in night game, then you will want to time constraint if you feel that you need to and then transition. A transition is when you move from the opening topic of conversation onto another topic of conversation. As the man, it is your responsibility to keep the conversation moving forward so you should always have some default way to do this prepared. Not having a transitional sound bite memorized is the Number One reason why a conversation won't go further than the opener. A few examples of how to transition well are:

"What's the occasion tonight?"

"Who has the best outfit on tonight?"

"You guys aren't English, are you?"

"Which one of you is the boss? There is always one leader in any social group."

"Do you live here or are you on holiday?

Once you have transitioned you can talk about any topic of conversation. If you feel nervous, tongue-tied, or stressed, then tell her. Remember that it's most attractive if you are authentic and not faking it. Also, for you to remove those feelings forever, you need to accept them and communicate them. You will only do more damage to yourself by learning a bunch of lines and trying to hide your emotions. You must heal and let go of these emotions first and then you will feel relaxed and comfortable using some of the lines and sound bites provided, and they will work better!

ATTRACTION

Have you ever seen a less-than-attractive man with a really beautiful woman? Maybe you've noticed this phenomenon in a bar or walking down the street. Attraction can be defined as: "If you believe you deserve the woman, then you will get her" or "If you believe you don't deserve the woman, then you won't get her." Both of these statements are true. Imagine walking up to a woman who you feel that you deserve. How would you feel, calm or stressed? Would you be loud or quiet? Standing straight or hunched? Would you have strong or weak eye contact?

The important thing is to approach the woman and assume that she will be attracted to you. This can be based on any reason. A lot of guys who are naturally good with women will have really bizarre reasons why women should be attracted to them. "I work out at the gym," "I'm good at sport," "I'm a DJ." Naturals will also often believe they are really good-looking, even when they are not. They just believe that they deserve the woman that they are approaching; it is no big deal to them!

The more success you get with women, the more you will start to believe in yourself. You will also want to be as positive as possible. Always be positive about the current situation and about how you are doing when you are out. Never be critical of yourself and when you get home think about the good approaches that you did and don't replay the worse ones. Be intelligent and make a change to your approach if you feel like you need to but never be critical of yourself.

Finally, before you approach the woman, imagine her naked in her bed last night masturbating whilst thinking of you. Really take a minute to imagine her lying on her bed and pleasuring herself whilst shouting out your name, "Kingy, Kingy, KINGY!!!" (Obviously, insert your own name here.) Then make your approach! If you have properly imagined this and put yourself in this state, you will approach a lot more calmly with an almost "I know what you did last night, you naughty girl" look on your face. This is called assuming attraction when you approach, knowing that the woman wants you and it is up to you to test if you are compatible or not.

It is also important in an interaction to have a few sound bites that you can use to generate attraction. Let's say, techniques to spice it up occasionally. The following are lines and techniques you can use to do this.

"High-Five"

The high-five is a great way to increase touch between you and the girl, and it also generates attraction. It shows that you are a fun guy and not serious and boring.

"Do you spin?"

After you high-five her, it is good to then ask, "Do you spin?" with your hand up, then take her hand and spin her round. If she looks cold or that she doesn't want to spin, then don't force her. Once she has spun and you are still holding her hand, say "No I meant the other way," then spin her round in the other direction. Spinning women is a fantastic way to generate quick attraction in the woman and get her to have fun with you. You can spin her at any point in a conversation just by asking "do you spin?".

"I love you but I hate you."

A great natural way to increase attraction is to do something that is called push-pull. This is when you say something nice and then you give her a tease. For example:

"You are either the coolest girl ever, or a complete dork."

"I love your smile, but your teeth are funny."

"I don't know if I love you or I hate you yet."

"I love your dress. I saw a girl wearing exactly the same one a minute ago."

"I love you... get away from me."

The format is:

One generic or specific compliment + One generic or specific tease

You can create you own push-pull when you are out. If she is wearing a hat, then you could say "I love your hat, it reminds me of Indiana Jones." Use your creativity and remember that the compliment and tease don't even have to relate to each other. Saying, "Your hair is great but your nails suck," works just as well even though the two things don't relate.

When you do a push-pull you should calibrate how muchthe woman reacts to you. Most women will know that you are just playing with them and like it. A few women wont like push-pull and might get upset if the tease is too strong. If she looks offended then you will want to smile and say, "I like that." This little calibration at the end prevents her from getting angry and makes her feel good again.

Don't use the push-pull technique too much; no more than once or twice during your approach. The main bulk of your attraction should come from having the alpha qualities of confidence, humor, positivity, and state transfer (see pages 145-149), and kino escalation (see pages 150-151). Any techniques should be used sparingly and not as a substitute for real conversation. Use this technique a couple of times during your conversation to give her some emotions and keep the interaction on a fun sexual level.

Chapter 11:
Become A Master
Anticipator

When you are in conversation with a woman be prepared to prevent problems from occurring. With infield experience you will cultivate a sixth sense. You won't see dead people, but you will be able to predict what is going to happen next. Become a master anticipator in all situations and apply a remedy as required.

If you see a woman with a big smile on her face moving toward your target, anticipate an interruption. Immediately turn to your target and say, "Don't be rude, introduce me to your friend." You don't want her friend to interrupt the conversation and then you stand there looking glum until the friend leaves.

If you feel that your target is going to move away or she says that she has to go, then you use a time constraint, "I can only stay for a few minutes because I'm meeting my friend Candy for a coffee." Problem solved. She will now stay a little longer because of that imposed time constraint.

Does being a master anticipator not conflict with being in the present moment and the power of now? Good question. Action always comes from the present moment. Whatever you do always comes from the now. Being an anticipator does not mean you worry about all of the negative things that could go wrong in the interaction. It also doesn't mean that you spend time in the future. A master anticipator will recognize patterns of behavior in the now. For example, I won't imagine the woman wants to leave because I'm such a boring person. Instead I might notice that she appears distracted or that she's unsettled or in a rush. Then I will quickly deliver the time constraint to prevent the "I have to go" from coming up.

BE OBLIVIOUS TO HER REACTIONS

Often women will be indifferent to your approach, sometimes even mean. You are no big deal to most women and they will usually forget about you within minutes of you walking away. This is a huge concept for a lot of students to grasp as they really worry about the woman's opinion of them.

A good rule of thumb is that you should be willing to do 90 percent of the talking for the first few minutes. Remember that a woman's attraction is based on your behavior, so it takes a little time for her to feel attracted. When you say something funny, do something dominant, or display another alpha-male characteristic. Then attraction will happen.

Don't look at her initial reaction to you; just have fun and continue talking for your own amusement. Have confidence that most women do like you when they get to know you. She may have closed body language or be looking away, but just continue talking and be a bit persistent. Usually, as you continue talking you will say something that she likes or responds to, then opens up. Don't forget, she could be your future girlfriend. Continue talking and push the interaction a bit further.

If she tells you to go away or walks off, then reject her politely and go back to your friends, or talk to another group of people.

If the woman isn't feeling entitled herself or isn't in a social mood she will react badly to your approach. If this is the situation, keep talking until she opens up or tells you to leave.

STATE TRANSFER

Do you want to know the secret to my game? State transfer. Simply put this means: what you feel, the woman will feel. I'm talking about something that is very alien to most men not involved in the pick-up community—emotions.

Women pick up on emotions and the vibe of an interaction a lot better than men do. They do this because the words aren't that important to them. Through evolution women have learned that men can lie about things.

In most Hollywood films there is a good guy and a bad guy. The film Aladdin springs to mind because I was made to watch it a few days ago (I have to admit that I do like the songs). Can you imagine the sorcerer, with his angry and sinister vibes, approaching you on the street and asking you for money for an orphanage that he is building for blind children? It would seem unlikely that a guy like that would have the compassion to care about the welfare of others. He has a "the world hurt me when I was younger and I don't fit in so I'm going to get my own back, you wait and see" vibe.

That can be what it is like for women because they can usually read and feel the vibes a lot better than we do. If any angry guy approaches a woman in a bar and in a passive-aggressive tone asks for advice about what gift he can buy for his niece, the approach probably isn't going to work. You need to develop positive, peaceful, or even sexual emotions and approach while feeling these.

There are lots of possible states and emotions that you can feel but the main ones are fear, sexual, and peace. Remember that it is important to accept and communicate whatever state you are in even if it is a negative one. If you do this, then the negative state will disappear more quickly and it will be less likely to return in the future too.

FEAR

Fear is a negative state and comes from the mind being in the future and not the present moment. In the present moment, even if you are about to approach a woman, everything is good. You are standing there or walking toward her—nothing bad is happening right then. The mind loves to try to predict things and think: "What will happen if I approach her?" and you might end up making some negative predictions which are false. You always want to stay in the present moment and meditation, a healthy diet, and expanding your comfort zone will help with this. If you find yourself in a negative state like fear, then take on the maybe attitude of "maybe I am feeling fear right now." Accepting it and not identifying with it is the best way for it to pass. What you resist will persist.

SEXUAL

Sexual is a positive state and one that can be fun to play around with. Being in a sexual state will create sexual attraction in the woman very quickly if she is open to it. It is a state that speeds up the seduction process and can achieve really quick results with women, even all the way to the bedroom. It is not uncommon for you to be able to get sexual with each other within just a few minutes of meeting her. Some women will be open to it, some women will enjoy feeling those sexual vibes but not be open to it that night, and other women just won't be open to it. You can switch on the sexual state in the middle of a pick-up when you feel it necessary.

The best way to put yourself in a sexual state is to imagine a past girlfriend who gave you the best sex you ever had, or think of your favorite porn video before you make the approach. Take a few seconds to really visualize and then make the approach.

During the interaction you can also visualize the woman that you are talking to doing something sexual. As soon as you start to feel aroused, then she will feel it too. This may or may not be noticeable. The signs are usually her displaying more interest in what you are saying, although I have given women mini-orgasms while approaching them on the street in a sexual state. One attractive woman dropped her bags when she felt those emotions during my approach. I got her number shortly afterward and saw her that night. This is not the norm, but being able to put yourself in a sexual state is a useful tool for any pick-up artist to have.

PEACE

Peace should be your default state. This might seem passive and not very exciting, but this could not be further from the truth. Being peaceful means that you fully accept the moment and that you aren't carrying any guilt, anger, or resentment. By being peaceful and in a state of full acceptance you will put the woman in a state of full acceptance, too. She will accept the interaction you are having because you are accepting it. This means that the majority of the time she will stop and listen to you.

In addition to this, being in a state of peace also communicates really high value. It communicates that you have your life together and that you aren't damaged. A guy with mother issues or who was bullied as a child won't be approaching a woman in a state of peace. Only a cool guy who loves himself and the people around him would be like this. Let me be clear that I had mother issues and was bullied as a child. This peaceful state can be cultivated through love, compassion, and acceptance for yourself and others. That sounds so hippy, but if it works it works, right?

If you aren't currently a peaceful person and have some negative vibes or blockages, then you will need to work on accepting those first to remove them. If you get nervous, shy, frustrated, stressed, or angry when talking to women, then your outer game should take a back seat for a month or two and you should work on your inner game. I know a couple of months sounds like a long time but wouldn't it be worth it to never get those feelings again for the rest of your life?

So, if you think this might apply to you on some level, it definitely did to me, then you need to start being really honest with yourself about how you feel when approaching women. If you feel shy when talking to a woman, then tell her, "Hey, I'm feeling pretty shy right now." If you are feeling frustrated, then tell her, "Hey, I'm feeling a bit frustrated."

This self-acceptance is key and tells your internal body that this problem is no big deal. Through this acknowledgement and acceptance the problem's power over you will weaken until it doesn't exist anymore. Turn your focus inward even during the pick-up and see what is happening. Don't place meaning on it, just observe it, and then tell the woman, "I'm feeling angry." Women can make some of the best counselors, they are free, and hot! Also, if you are feeling bad the woman probably knows anyway so it is actually cool to communicate this because it shows you know how to deal with things.

We aren't meant to be perfect. It is OK to feel bad sometimes. The acceptance of those things you might not like feeling will mean they will return less and less, until they don't return at all. By being an imperfect human you are demonstrating that you are real, authentic, and aware of the natural flow of life. People will like you and want to be around that. People like to see something real. I don't know about you, but whenever something seems manufactured or manipulated, I switch off.

BE CHEEKY

A very useful frame and tone for your interactions with women is to be cheeky. The word cocky gets used a lot, which is OK, but I think there is a definite difference between "cocky" and "cheeky." Being cocky comes from the place of feeling better than the person you are talking to. There is a fine line between confidence and arrogance, and a lot of women will be offended if you are cocky.

Being cheeky is a much more playful way of expressing yourself than being cocky. To be cheeky means that you are essentially making the comment for your own amusement. You aren't trying to be mean; you're just having a bit of playful fun. When I say the word "cheeky," what images enter your head? What about when I say the word "cocky"? The images are different aren't they? One of the images in my mind in connection with the word "cheeky" is a boy sticking out his tongue at a girl. You want to be a lot of things and cheeky, confident, and sexual are great places to start. Being cheeky usually comes with a smile, which allows you to calibrate the tease by showing warmth to the person you're with.

KINO ESCALATION—HOW TO TOUCH PROPERLY

Newborn babies and children need to be touched all the time, otherwise their behavior becomes angry and aggressive. If a newborn is deprived of touch for too long they develop long-term psychological trauma. As we get older we develop coping mechanisms to deal with a loss of physical contact. However, we all love and need human touch.

Kino escalation should happen during the day and night. During the day you will want to touch about 70 percent less than at night. The secret to touching is for you to be confident and sure about what you are doing. You just want to be normal about it, think what a cool touchy-feely guy would be like. Obviously, if you have little experience in touching a woman then imagining this is easier said than done. Instead think about guys such as Robbie Williams or Russell Brand, both very touchy-feely guys.

Never look where you are touching, as this will put pressure on the situation. Instead, have your arms bent and you will find that you naturally gesture, as you would with a friend. To increase sensations when you touch, it's good to touch gently and use your fingernails. Try this now: take your fingernails and very lightly run them over the inner part of your arm and your inner elbow. If you are doing this right it should feel very nice (in Borat voice).

Your touch should escalate gradually. I'm not going to list a ten-step structure on how to escalate touch with a woman; thinking too much about something will only mess things up. Instead, be aware that some parts of a woman's body are much more intimate than others. That said, you can pretty much touch a woman anywhere as long as you are confident about it and you don't linger. An example of how to escalate touch might be to start with lightly touching her shoulders and arms; then her belly, legs, or hands; finally working your way to the hair, neck, and lips.

It is important to calibrate to her comfort levels. For example, if she responds well to your touch, then this is a good sign. If she looks uncomfortable, then stop touching and continue talking. When she is laughing or looking more comfortable you can escalate again. Keep repeating this process: escalate, back up, try and escalate again. The more you touch, the more attraction will increase in the woman. If women walk away during your interactions, then you are not meeting their emotional needs. Check to make sure that you are escalating your kino and you haven't gone for long periods of chat with no touch.

A super-kino move is to pick the woman up mid-conversation and then spin her round in a fun way. You obviously need to calibrate to the vibe of the room. This move creates massive attraction and really accelerates an interaction toward a more sexual level. To understand how to do it properly, it is best to see a professional doing this infield.

HOW TO TELL STORIES FOR VALUE

I remember one time when I went to the yard to hang out some laundry, an older guy from my apartment block was talking to some women through the window. He was confident and the women were laughing, so naturally this piqued my interest. In the middle of the conversation he started telling them how hot his ex-girlfriend was and that she used to model for Vogue. The women went silent. He then continued to persuade them that it was true and he even had photos he could show them. Silence from the women, followed by a weak smile. He was getting even more frustrated and was actually about to go inside and up to his room to find these photos when they said, "It's OK, we have to go now." And with a polite "Nice to meet you" and a weak smile they went back into their apartment.

So what happened? Ironically, the guy was doing really well until he brought up the story about his ex-girlfriend modelling for Vogue. In itself it wasn't a bad thing to say; in fact, it was a very cool thing to say. It's just that it came out as if he was trying to impress them. This is called "qualifying yourself" to someone; you don't believe who you are is coming through so you go out of your way to impress that person.

The fact is, he probably did date a Vogue model. He seemed cool to me, but his sub-communications messed up the interaction. It is low-value to try to impress someone and you should never try too hard to impress. It is OK to tell cool stories about yourself because you are enjoying telling the story but it is not cool to tell a story in order to impress someone. A guy who always dates models wouldn't even mention it. Why would he? It's just the norm.

So the lesson is, don't ever try to impress another person or say things that imply another person should be impressed. You think that saying these things will demonstrate value but instead they lower your value because you are "trying." This is also true for playing games or doing magic tricks for women. If the woman is smiling and interested in you it's usually better to move on to qualification or rapport (see pages 159–161). By staying in the attraction phase when the woman is already attracted to you, you risk subliminally communicating that you don't think you are good enough. This is very common with good-looking guys or guys who want to fit the woman's stereotypical type. If you are using humor and running attraction material for your own amusement, then this is different. You maintain your value because you are sub-communicating that you aren't looking to impress the woman but just having fun.

To avoid seeming like you are trying to impress the woman, demonstrate value in the middle of the conversation and not at the end. So instead of "My girlfriend used to model for Vogue," and then there's a pause while you look for a reaction, say something like "I remember once when I was flying to Spain with my ex-girlfriend, don't hate her but she had a modeling gig for Vogue and I was traveling with her for the free vacation. Anyway, we were sitting in the middle aisle with the four seats next to each other and an old woman fell asleep on my shoulder..." Why is this better than the first example? It's better because you

continue talking after demonstrating value. So, instead of looking for a reaction when you said your ex used to model for Vogue, you continue talking. This sub-communicates that hot women are interested in you, but that you don't find this particularly important. And because you don't find this important, it implies that this happens to you all the time.

When talking to a woman of average looks, don't talk about Vogue models. You will make women who aren't that confident about their looks feel bad about themselves, and they'll then view you negatively for making them feel that way. Conversely, if you tell a story about your average ex-girlfriend to a hot woman she will view herself as being superior to you and that you aren't an alpha male. When you get to the stage of knowing you can quite easily go out and get a hot girlfriend you won't mention these things at all. It is obvious to the woman by seeing you talk to other women that you are a cool guy.

Be aware that you can also communicate low value in stories through the actual words that you say. For instance, telling a story about how your ex-girlfriend dumped you is never good. The same applies to stories about how you got beaten up or how you were really shy and embarrassed on a certain occasion. These are all negative stories. If your value is really high in the woman's eyes, then you can get away with a few of these stories. If your value isn't that high, then it's a good rule of thumb to avoid telling a woman about any negative representation of the alpha-male characteristics.

Never lie when telling stories but always be proud of what you have done and who you have dated. Being honest with yourself will build self-esteem and confidence.

Chapter 12:
Qualification

Qualification comes after the woman shows signs that she is attracted to you. It allows you to find out things about her. Female to male attraction has to come first because it takes women a little time to feel attraction. Female attraction is like a volume knob that responds to your behavior and gets turned up by alpha-male demonstrations.

So, demonstrate your personality first and then when she is showing interest you can begin qualification.

Take five minutes to write down three things that you look for in a woman that aren't about her looks. That way, when you ask one of these questions, the woman will notice that you legitimately care about the answer. If you run out of things to say, I recommend you ask a qualification question. These questions are a lot more interesting than talking about the weather, which just looks like you are filling time.

When you ask a qualification question you should ask it in a slightly judgmental tone. Many times on boot camp, I see students asking qualification questions in an attempt to develop rapport. You shouldn't be asking these questions if you're just going to agree with whatever she says.

The tone you use to say things will make a big difference to how they are interpreted. When talking you will always be in one of these three types of rapport:

TR = Trying for rapport

NR = Neutral rapport

BR = Breaking rapport

You can see that TR slopes up at the end, which refers to the pitch of your voice increasing at the end of a sentence. NR is neutral, so the pitch of your voice doesn't fluctuate. The pitch of your voice lowers at the end of a sentence in BR. This might be how your boss talks to you. You want to be talking in either NR or BR and never in TR. Trying comes from a place of lower value and a lacking of abundance.

Qualification usually comes in the form of a statement and a question.

Statement:

"I find I get on well with people who like to travel."

This sets the tone and makes it clear what you like.

Question:

"Do you like to travel?"

This is the qualification and she now has a choice. She can either try to impress you with "Yes I love traveling" or "No, not really", which would mean that the qualification didn't work. If she doesn't qualify herself, then it usually means that there isn't enough attraction and you'll have to go back to the attraction phase and try the qualification phase later, when you have more attraction.

If the woman doesn't qualify herself, then you can punish her slightly by paying her less attention. Look around the room, turn your back to her, and talk to her friends, or just look a little disappointed. You don't want to be happy with everything that she says. If the woman annoys or disappoints you, show this. Then go back to attraction by expressing your personality naturally, and then try another qualification question. Repeat this process until the woman qualifies herself or walks off.

If the woman does qualify herself, then reward this with attention. Touching her on the arm, hand, or shoulder and then saying "I knew you were cool" are always good.

Alternatively, express interest in what she is saying and at the end say, "That's awesome. I love that," and then proceed to another topic of conversation.

Example

Man: "I tend to find I get on with people who like to travel or at least would be willing to travel. Do you like to travel?"

Woman: "Yes I like to travel, I went to the USA for three months."

Man: "That's awesome, what part of the USA did you go to?"

Woman: "I backpacked down the west coast all the way to Mexico."

Man: "I love traveling, I knew you were cool."

(Man returns to normal conversation and vibing.)

You now have something in common and have increased your connection with each other. Qualification also reduces last-minute resistance in the bedroom. I have found that even if the woman isn't into traveling, or whatever you asked about, but she is attracted to you, she will usually find some way to impress you.

BOUNDARIES

The feminine enjoys testing the masculine to see if he is being authentic and knows what he wants. This isn't a conscious behavior; it's sub-conscious. If you are empty and at one with life, then very little reaction will take place within you. This is a demonstration of an attractive masculine quality. By not reacting and passing tests like these, you'll increase the woman's attraction for you.

It is important that you recognize where to draw the line when the woman is making bad decisions. Use your own common sense. If she is exhibiting a behavior that you don't like and this is causing you tension, then tell her. Tell her this behavior is not something that is OK and do so from a positive but firm place. You are telling her this because you want what is best for her and for you. Be aware of what you are subliminally saying, though. If you are telling her not to talk to other men, then this might seem unreasonably jealous and that you don't think that you are enough. On the other hand, if she is flirting with other guys and touching them, then she needs to know that you're not OK with it.

Some women are damaged and are unable to change their behavior. You then have to decide if you are willing to accept this in the relationship. It is possible to rewire anyone's beliefs and outlook but it does take time, sometimes years. You have to decide whether you are prepared to sacrifice your time and energy. Personally, I like to make sure a woman has high self-esteem and a good sense of humor early on in any interaction. I'll do this by being cheeky and sexual to see if she can take teasing and has a sense of humor. If she gets offended, then we probably aren't going to get on anyway.

ISOLATION

It is great to be in the moment, not thinking and just having fun, but as the man you must be leading. A man knows what he wants and goes for it. When you have been in conversation for a while, lead the woman you like to a more intimate part of the venue—shops, pubs, bars, clubs—any venue can be suitable for a successful isolation. Ideally it should be quiet enough to talk, and away from the visual stimulation of, say, the dance floor in a club. Then, once isolated, you can build more connection and escalate touch with each other. I recommend no more than kissing. An isolation is like a mini-date. Every new location you visit together will build trust—she'll feel increasingly safe in your company.

The best way to isolate a woman is to ask her friends if you can borrow her for a little while. Point to where you are taking her and tell her friends they can join you in a few minutes if they want. The main issue that women have when you ask them to join you in a new location is they worry about what their friends think. If you ask her friends first and they are OK with it, then chances are she will be fine with it too.

I recommend that you try to isolate the woman you like in every approach that you make. Have it in your mind before you approach: where are you going to isolate her to? As long as you try, it will be a success. There is no failure, only feedback. Isolation is not about you separating her and making her feel vulnerable. Instead it is used to build connection and trust.

BUILDING COMFORT AND RAPPORT

Rapport is important in an interaction. Without it, the odds of seeing that person again are pretty low. People look to confirm their view of reality. This means that they want to surround themselves with people who view the world in a similar way—"If other people view the world in the same way as me, then this means that my beliefs are correct. This person really understands me."

To create rapport, establish commonalities between the two of you. To build rapport the woman must be attracted to you in some way, or at least respect you. If you look to build commonalities too early, then she usually won't answer the questions. Remember, attraction in women is like a volume knob, so a lot of this comes down to giving something a try and, if it's too early, try again later. There is no rejection, only feedback that she is not ready yet.

If the woman is showing signs of attraction, look to build comfort. Here's a list of the main ways that you can do this:

- **Take an interest in her life (job, friends, hobbies, family)**

- **Find commonalities (shared interests and experiences)**

- **Share vulnerabilities (show her that you are a real person)**

- **Win peer approval (her friends and family like you)**

- **Experience activities together (you start to create a story together)**

- **Lead her through a range of emotions (shows that you understand her)**

- **Do what you say you will (this builds trust, shows that you don't lie)**

- **Remove her from uncomfortable situations (shows you understand her)**

I stress that comfort should only be built once attraction is in place. If you try to build rapport before the woman is showing signs of attraction you demonstrate low value: "the nice guy." A high-value guy with many options wouldn't be interested in building rapport with a woman he doesn't know anything about. So, attract the woman first and then qualify her before moving on to the comfort stage.

However, if you are at a party within your social circle, then you will probably want to start at the comfort stage. Knowing things like this only really comes with social intuition and having experienced rejection many times before. Never worry about rejection as this will consciously and subconsciously improve your social calibration for the next time. Doing nothing really is the worst possible option.

Even in the comfort stage you should maintain that attractive vibe you had previously. This should be done by continuing to demonstrate alpha-male qualities: confidence, humor, dominance. Touching should also be present—long periods of time without it could land you in the "let's just be friends" zone.

Comfort usually happens in isolation when the two of you are away from the rest of the social group. In a group situation the vibe usually has a lot more social banter, which is not suitable for having a deep conversation. Use your own intuition to judge if you want to isolate or wait for a later point to build comfort with the woman.

When you find a strong commonality it can often transform a boring interaction into glory. Once I approached an attractive brunette woman during the day and we were having a nice chat. There was a bit of teasing and she was laughing but there was no real spark. The conversation was nice but the energy was low between us. I then asked her what she liked to do for fun and she said that she liked reading a lot at the moment. This didn't make me think "Wow," but then she mentioned that she was reading a popular self-help book. Instinctively my response was, "Oh my God, I love that book! How did you get into that stuff?" We then started finding commonalities about the book and related topics. My passion for talking about self-help was contagious and we had an amazing conversation. I got her number and we both left feeling we had found someone that really understood the other. I followed up with a simple text message starting with "Hey crazy Tony Robbins girl :-p (text emoticon for a cheeky face with a tongue stuck out)" and fade to black, times of passion.

INVESTING

I want you to imagine saving for an amazing vacation to the Canary Islands. You work all year, get a second job, and save really hard so you can afford it. However, one week before your vacation you win a trip to the Canary Islands for the exact same week that the vacation you've paid for is booked. There is no refund or exchange available and only you and your girlfriend can travel as they are the names on the tickets. Which tickets do you think you will want to use to travel? The ones you won in the competition or the ones that you worked all year to purchase?

I think most of us would agree that we'd want to use the tickets that we worked for. The amount of time and effort that was invested into the tickets that were bought increases their value. This fundamental concept of investment is applicable to everything. The more you invest into something, the more value you presume it has.

Now, if you were to offer both sets of tickets to a stranger, which ones do you think they would take? It would probably be fifty-fifty. So what is the hidden value that only we can see? It's our investment.

Be aware of the amount of time and effort that you invest into a woman. If you are in a relationship it is good to make a fair level of investment. However, if you invest too much, she will become needy and you could end up with a possessive woman.

Looking at photographs or daydreaming about a woman you like will only place more hidden value on her. Why? Because you are investing your time and emotions. None of it is real; it is just in your mind, but that hidden value will feel real to you and you'll end up acting differently around her. You'll try not to say something silly or start being a bit clingy and in turn drive the woman away. Even reading this book will increase women's value to you because you are investing both your time and money to learn about dating. Always bear this in mind: a guy who doesn't really care about what he says is a lot more attractive than one who is trying too hard.

So, if investing too much in something makes us go silly and prevents us being our real selves, then what does it do to women? It makes them do exactly the same things; they feel shy and clingy. The more a woman invests in you, the more she will want things to work between the two of you.

A woman won't invest in you unless she is attracted to you first, though. This attraction comes from demonstrating that you have alpha-male characteristics. Investments initially start off small and then gradually increase in size over time. Below are examples of different sizes of investments and when they are appropriate.

Before sex—small investments

- **She buys you a drink**

- **She meets you for a date**

- **She speaks to you on the phone**

- **She buys you a little present, worth no more than $1.50 (£1)**

- **She spends time with you**

- **She reveals an insecurity to you**

- **She qualifies herself to you**

- **She looks you up on Facebook**

After sex—medium investments increasing to large investments

• **She pays for dinners**

• **She gets jealous when she sees you interact with other women**

• **She pays for transport to visit you**

• **She buys you a present**

• **She reveals sexual desires to you**

• **She introduces you to her friends**

• **She introduces you to her parents**

Investment can come in many different forms, but usually it's in the form of time, emotion, or finance. Investment is basically just getting someone to do something for you. People can either invest because you ask them to or they do it on their own. For instance, you could ask a woman to buy you a drink. This is something that you are asking the woman to do, you are asking her to invest. Alternatively, the woman could look you up on Facebook and then send you an e-mail. Here the woman is investing of her own accord.

I stress again that you don't want the woman to invest too much in you, otherwise you will get an extremely clingy woman. In a relationship it is good to be fair, just be aware if you are investing too much into something.

If you aren't yet in a relationship, then it is always a good idea to get the woman investing as much as possible. Getting a woman to buy you a drink when you meet her in a bar will result in a much higher probability of you seeing her again. Why? You probably know the answer to this already. She has more invested in you and so rationalizes that you must be a cool guy. She would only buy a drink for a cool guy and so you must have been special.

Chapter 13:
Cold Reading

A great natural tool that any aspiring pick-up artist should have in his arsenal is cold reading. Cold reading is a technique used by pick-up artists to build both attraction and comfort by demonstrating that he knows something about the woman he is trying to pick up without any prior knowledge. A successful cold read will lead the girl to feel a closer connection to you. We all like to assert our own realities and when people are telling us things that do this we automatically agree with them.

"I'd imagine your friends are very important to you."

"I can tell you are a social person."

"I can tell inner qualities are much more important to you then external things."

These are examples of generic cold reads that I might make on a woman. Most women are going to agree with those statements. When the woman agrees with a statement, then she is acknowledging that you understand her on that level. A really good cold read will make you the most interesting guy the woman has met this year, if not ever. People are really most interested in themselves and a great way to talk about the other person is through cold reading. A cold reading should start on general topics but gradually start opening up to more deep topics. A deep topic is usually one that involves emotional attachment—a few examples are past relationships, family, sexual experiences, and school experiences.

If, instead of cold reading you ask questions, such as "Are your friends important to you?" the woman will probably respond with "Why" or just give an answer. The problem with this is that you aren't really demonstrating that you understand her. Also most guys will ask generic questions like this, very rarely will a man cold read a woman.

Cold reading also allows you to teach the woman something about herself. This teaching frame will give you authority over her world. It will also give you lots of call-back humor that you can add into future text messages or conversation. For example, if you find out that her most embarrassing moment was treading in dog poop, then you can playfully text her: "Hey crazy dog poop girl :-p"

The structure for cold reading is that you make statements and then look for her response. If the response is positive then you continue with "and." If the response is negative, then you continue with "but." See the example below.

"I can tell your friends are very important to you..."

(She nods.)

"...and you have one best friend that you tell all your secrets to..."

(She shakes her head.)

"...but rather than one best friend you do have people you can confide in."

(She nods her head.)

So, it's "and" for a positive response and "but" for a negative response. You can do this for as long as you want. If you get the first few guesses correct, then usually the woman will buy into the rest of the cold read. I recommend that you try to cold read every woman that you talk to. During the day do less cold reading, it is a little too weird unless you're sat down in a coffee shop. Stick to just a couple of guesses. It's better to cold read in a quiet place with few distractions, and it's preferable if you're sitting down.

NUMBER CLOSING

There will come a time during the interaction when you will want to enact a venue change. This is not always possible as sometimes the woman or you might be in a rush. In this case you will want to get what in London we call her "digits," meaning her phone number.

There are two ways of getting her phone number. You can either make solid plans, or it can be a lot more casual. If you have shared over 20 minutes together you're safe to make it solid.

SOLID NUMBER CLOSE

The reason for getting her number should be based on something you have in common. Having found this out during the qualification stage, this becomes the reason to see each other again.

Example One

Man: "I want to check out this cool bar in Soho sometime. Do you like cocktails?"

Woman: "Yes, I love them."

Man: "Cool, the bar is meant to be amazing. It has live music. What would be the best way of getting in contact with you, so we can check it out sometime?"

(Woman will then either give you her e-mail address, tell you to contact her through Facebook, or give you her phone number.)

Usually she will give you her e-mail address if she has a boyfriend, tell you to contact her through Facebook if she needs to get to know you better, and she'll give you her phone number if she is feeling comfortable about the idea of seeing you again. Obviously these rules are not set in stone. There have been many occasions when an e-mail has led to amazing nights of passion.

Example Two

Man: "What do you like to do in your spare time?"

Woman: "I love going to art galleries."

Man: "No way! That's cool. What type of art are you most into?"

(Conversation develops.)

So, using the above example, when it comes to the time to get her digits, her love of art galleries is the reason you'd use for this. This commonality increases your bond and there will be a lot more chance of you seeing each other again. The reason shouldn't be sex. Her emotional state will change when she leaves the club, she will rationalize that you just wanted sex, and she won't want to meet up.

Example Two continued

Man: "Cool, well, I've got to go and meet a friend but let's check out the National Gallery one day next week. What would be the best way of getting in contact with you?"

(Woman will then either give you her e-mail address, tell you to contact her through Facebook, or give you her phone number.)

Obviously, if you aren't into art galleries, then don't make this the reason to see each other. It's always best to find things that you genuinely have in common because then your enthusiasm will be transparent.

CASUAL NUMBER CLOSE

Sometimes you just won't have time to build a solid connection with the woman. In this case you want to open, quickly qualify on something light, and then go for a casual number close. Although this may result in her giving you a fake phone number, there is still some chance you will see her again. It is actually not a bad approach and taking this approach with ten women might lead to three meeting up with you again.

Example One

Man: "I'm actually in a bit of a rush, I'm meeting my friends Katie and Sarah for coffee but I liked this conversation. You have a good energy about you. Enter your number and maybe we can go for a coffee some time? I can only take it if it's an English number though."

Woman: "Yes it's a English number."

Man: "Cool, 07..."

What is happening here is you are mentioning that you are off to meet a couple of female friends, which shows you must be a cool guy. You say that you like her energy—this becomes the reason to see each other again. This is called false qualifying—you indicate that she has matched up to your standards without actually asking her a question. Finally, you say, "I can only take your number if it's an English number." This is called a distracter. She is agreeing it's a UK number, but you presume she is agreeing to see you again, so you then prompt her to enter her number.

Example Two

Man: "I'm actually in a bit of a rush, I'm meeting my friends Katie and Sarah for coffee but I liked this conversation. You seem interesting. I organize parties and the last one we had was a pub crawl of the Monopoly board; it's a lot of fun. Lots of women and cool guys get together. What's your number and I'll send you a text about when the next one is. You are welcome to bring friends."

(Woman enters her number.)

This is a very casual number close but it is very effective if you are looking to build your social circle. Saying she is welcome to bring friends will remove the pressure that it will be an awkward date. If she turns up with a couple of female friends, awesome. You will be pre-selected for the whole night (see pages 32–34).

KISS CLOSE

In any interaction with a woman there is always a risk and reward scheme. Just like investing money, the bigger the risk that you take, the bigger the potential reward. In the dating world I have discovered that it is a lot better to make a move and fail than to not make a move at all. The woman will actually find it a lot more attractive that you went for it rather than being too scared. Often times gentlemen will wait until the end of the night, then go for an awkward kiss by the car, when there has been no flirting or touching during the rest of the date. I imagine it would feel like a terrible and awkward moment with a drunk cousin.

Instead, keep things sexual. Touch throughout the night. Move your face toward her for a second and then move it back. Do this a few times and look to see if she maintains eye contact or if her pupils dilate. (Pupil dilation means the black part of the eye gets bigger. This only happens when someone is attracted to you or if they are really scared.) If she keeps eye contact, then go in for the kiss. The signs are she will be OK with it. If she looks the other way or looks uncomfortable, then this is a sign to pull back and continue talking: she isn't ready for the kiss yet.

Eye contact can also be very important when going for the kiss close. A useful tip is to use lots of eye contact when talking with her and if she is maintaining it, then this is positive. When you are talking to her, look at her eyes and then down to her lips and then back up to the eyes. Do this a few times. When people are about to kiss they will look at each others' lips and by doing this will activate her kissing circuits in her brain. Don't be a robot: remember everything should be natural and fluid and not like you are programming a computer. When you look at her eyes, then her lips, do it smoothly and naturally; try not to force things.

There is also the verbal approach to the kiss. Do this after a moment of shared eye contact, slow talking, and touch.

Man: "What would you do if I kissed you right now?"

Response 1:

Woman: "I'd kiss you back." — Kiss her

Response 2:

Woman: "I'm not sure."

Man: "Let's find out." — Kiss her

Response 3:

Woman: "I wouldn't let you."

Man: "I never said I was going to. It just looked like you had something on your mind."

Often times the woman will tell you what to do in order to kiss her; for instance, if she says:

"I can't kiss you here," move her to another part of the venue away from her friends and kiss here there.

"I can't kiss you now," then be cool about it and try for the kiss close a
little later on in the evening.

Don't go for the kiss during lots of laughter or during a discussion on a serious topic. It is best when there is a drop in conversation, or put your hand to her lips—"Shhhh"—and then ask the kiss question.

Another technique is to start accusing her of making you feel this way: "I'm trying so hard not to kiss you right now," or "Don't even look at me, seriously this is your fault," or "I've lost control of my mind." Do this once, look away from her for 30 seconds, and then continue conversation with her. Wait a few minutes and then go for the kiss close using the verbal approach listed above.

To get a quick kiss close, you want to get her very emotional quickly. You can do this by making her laugh and then pushing her away repeatedly:

Man: "Oh my God, you remind me of a fan of Sex in the City."

Woman: "Ha ha ha."

Man: "Get away from me. I hate you, leave me alone."

or "Only joking, come back here and have a little cuddle."

or "You are the devil, get away from me, ahhhh."

or "Only joking, come here, come here."

(Then kiss.)

This is a huge emotional rollercoaster. She was having a great time, then you tell her to leave you alone in a fun way. Actually, gently push her away while laughing and have fun with it. (Don't be serious or she will just go.) Her emotional circuits will go into overload and she will be a lot more likely to kiss you.

HOW TO MASTER THE DATE

A good date is one that moves your relationship forward. Let's look at the major rules for having a good date.

1. Lead—As a man it is your responsibility to plan and organize the date. Never ask the woman what she wants to do. Instead just presume she will like what you have in mind. This might sound a bit rude but women find this behavior very attractive. Being the feminine, the emotion, she just wants to experience something and not logically decide on anything.

2. Your turf—When going on a date arrange to meet her near your house. Unless you are in a relationship you never want to make too much effort to see her. Let her come to you. A great plan is to meet her at a coffee shop or bar near your house, then forget your wallet and have to go back for it. Let her come with you to get it, let her inside your house, grab your wallet, and then leave again. Don't try any escalation. The purpose of this is that when it comes to going back to yours later she will be less worried as she has been there already.

3. External stimulation—If your conversational skills aren't very strong, then take the woman somewhere where the pressure will be off the two of you. Drinks are OK if you are a good conversationalist, but there can be many awkward silences if you're not. A trip to an art gallery or shopping removes a lot of that social pressure of two strangers meeting up.

4. Multiple venues—It's a great idea to go to many different venues on your date. Sharing in multiple experiences together builds trust and will also give her more memories of the two of you. Increasing the amount of memories and experiences you've shared will make it seem like you've know each other for longer. Personally, I like to go on a bar crawl of the four bars on my street, the last one being very close to my house. We spend about one hour in each bar and, if the woman is comfortable, then we can go back to mine. If I sense she is not comfortable, then we can arrange another date in the future.

5. Emotions—Women love emotions and often experience a full range of them. Have a joke with her, play a game with her, have a deep conversation, tease her on her choice of shoes, tickle her, say something sexual. Try not to have too many logical conversations; instead it is always better to just make it fun for you. A woman doesn't usually feel strong attraction until she feels jealousy. You can manufacture jealousy by inviting multiple women to one venue. I have done this many times, inviting up to six women on one date with me. You'd think that they wouldn't be interested but instead they see you are pre-selected and they want you. It is then up to you to choose who you like or try to organize a threesome. Make sure everyone has a great time and the other women can always be invited out again at a later date.

6. Your friends—I have personally found that going on a date when the woman's friends will be there never works out well. It is always a little less comfortable. I'm having to be extra nice because her friends are there and she also feels judged by her friends for doing anything with me. Instead, reverse the situation and invite your friends out on the date too. Join your female friends with your date for drinks, as seeing you have women in your life already will increase attraction dramatically. A male wing can also be useful. He can meet you for an hour with his girlfriend and then go off and do his own thing. These things might seem scary to do and the first few times you might get it wrong, but with practice this way will make it a lot easier to win yourself those hot women.

7. Logistics—As you are the man, and you're leading, you need to handle the logistics. Be comfortable in the venue that you are going to. Know where you are going to go after this venue and make it seem spontaneous. How easy is it to get to your house from the last venue? If it is over a ten-minute journey, you might want to rethink it.

8. You—Make sure you arrange to see the woman when you are feeling good. Meeting the woman when you are stressed or ill is rarely going to make for a good date. If you are not at your best, then cancel the date and later on in the week organize another one. Canceling a date is so rare that the woman will assume you have a good life already and will be extra happy to see you the next time.

Good Date Examples

- **The park**

- **Cocktails**

- **Shopping**

- **Art gallery**

- **Festivals**

- **Amusement park**

Bad Date Examples

- **Movie theater**

- **Dinner**

- **House party where you don't know anyone**

KINO ESCALATION ON A DATE

It is important to set the correct frame of the date immediately, as soon as you see her. Do not bring her flowers or chocolates because this just makes you look desperate and supplicating. Instead, give her a kiss or a high-five and spin her around (see page 142). It is also good to make a cheeky comment, maybe about an item of clothing that she is wearing. For example, "I hate your shoes honey," said with a smile and done playfully will spike her emotions and shows you aren't intimidated or overthinking, you're just having fun. Also, you are mixing up the communication channels. Verbally you are saying that you hate her shoes, but you are smiling, which suggests that you don't really. This communication mix-up creates emotions and gets people investing into you by overthinking about what you just said. "Does he really hate my shoes or was he just playing with me?"

Touch the woman throughout the date. I don't mean poking her every couple of minutes but there shouldn't be long periods of time where no touching is going on. Kino is king and it increases attraction. Touching also shows the woman that you are a sexual being and you aren't going to be her gay best friend.

You can kiss the woman or not, that is your choice. If you do kiss her, then make sure the kissing doesn't progress into foreplay. Making out is fine as long as your hands don't start to wander. If you don't kiss the woman then that is OK too; just make it obvious that you are sexually interested in her. You can verbally escalate and kino escalate without the kiss and build up sexual tension between the two of you. For example, show her how to play pool or play on one of the dance arcade games together. Giving her a hug for a bit longer than you should or looking at her lips will also make her start to think about sex. Follow the verbal and physical escalation phases (see pages 79 and 150–151), but don't get into foreplay until you are back in the bedroom.

PAYING FOR THE DATE

To keep it really simple: if you would do it for your friend, then it is OK to do it on the date. So, for instance, if your friend drove an hour to see you, then maybe you would buy him a drink. If your friend lived close by, then maybe you would take it in turns to buy a round.

Some women have a rule that the man must pay on a date. Other women will want to pay their way and it's almost impossible to persuade them otherwise.

Don't make things awkward by saying "I won't pay for you" if she has no money. At the same time, don't pay for a lavish dinner. Generally you want the woman to invest money into the date, but if she can't or doesn't, then just be cool with it.

Chapter 14:
Statements of
Sexual Intent

Statements of sexual intent are used to set the frame of an interaction. They verbally acknowledge that the two of you might hook up tonight or at some point. I like to keep a conversation sexually charged for my own amusement and to screen to see if the woman is sexual. A woman who doesn't like sex will often not laugh at my humor and personally that is not a woman for me.

Below I've listed some statements of sexual intent. They are in order of shockability (low to high) and some of them are obviously not for use during the day.

- **"You notice how people in London look really sad, like you see them on the underground? Often I think, would it be OK to give them a bit of a cuddle? You could say come here and pop him on the breast."**

- **"It's you and me tonight."**

- **"I choose you."**

- **"You look flushed, are you ovulating today?"**

- **"I love your curves; they are really sexy. Don't show them to me dammit."**

- **"You, my darling, look like an adventure playground for my cock."**

- **"I'm trying so hard not to fuck you in the restroom right now."**

It is possible to use all of the these phrases in one conversation. These are some of the things that I find myself saying during an interaction with a woman. Mentioning that you love her curves will make the woman a lot less worried about you seeing her naked later.

Be aware that if it is not possible for you to take the woman that you are chatting to back to yours that night, then you should use less of these phrases. If you are going to have to meet her at another time, it is best to focus on comfort and rapport (see pages 159–161). If you are on a date and it is possible to go back to yours later, then using sexual humor is a good thing. For interactions during the day, express less sexual intent. In the evening you can express as much as you want.

Calibrate the woman's response. If she is giggling and laughing, then that is a positive sign. If she looks disgusted or annoyed, then don't react but lead on to other topics of conversation.

When you say something along the lines of the examples above and the woman stays, she is acknowledging that you and her could hook up. For instance, if you were to say, "It's you and me tonight" and she agrees, then she is logically accepting that you and her will hook up tonight.

Don't be afraid of expressing your sexuality, especially in a humorous way. Remember humor is all about setup and then surprise (see pages 38–39), so saying shocking things works in the same way. Avoid saying something sexual and then apologizing afterward by saying "only joking." This kills the sexual tension, but, if she looks genuinely upset, then obviously apologize. If she just looks a bit shocked, then don't worry; remember that women love experiencing different emotions.

If you aren't escalating either physically or sexually throughout the conversation, then the woman will feel a lot more awkward later. Be honest with your desires. Usually the woman will adapt to this. Don't be afraid to put yourself out there—remember, there is no failure, only feedback on your interaction. Women want to sleep with a sexually adventurous man and want a polite gentleman to babysit for them.

GETTING SEXUAL

So you've met this great woman and you want to take her back to your house. You want to bask in her beauty. You want to give yourself to her. You want her to give herself to you. As a man there is nothing more attractive than a woman truly in touch with her feminine. Full of life, it's almost as if sex dances across her face and her body. You can't help but be drawn to such a woman when you see her.

When having sex you are giving love and value, you aren't taking something, you are giving. This is a win-win scenario. You are helping the woman win, too. You are unlocking her body and heart through sexual dance.

When you are approaching a woman it should be because you want to and not because you think you should. I guarantee every time you see a hot woman, your core will shout "Yes." Focus on this voice rather than social conditioning. Allow yourself to enjoy the woman, but don't allow yourself to get distracted from your masculine presence. Enjoy her beauty, her voice, enjoy giving her different emotions, enjoy teasing her, enjoy the moment. Give yourself to her 90 percent of the way, then pull back 10 percent to demonstrate your willingness to walk away. You are enjoying the time you are spending with her, you like women, but she is not the only thing in your life. When you're in this state, being sexual with each other is a given—of course, this is going to happen tonight.

We sometimes get disconnected from our sexual side because we are taught to be gentlemen or that women don't like sex. We lose that primal instinct and joy in sex that allows us to feel free. This is the same for a one-night stand. A woman wants to be enjoyed, taken, and filled up from a place of love. Don't just follow a routine of pushing the woman up against your bedroom wall and kissing her. This can be a great thing to do, but do it because you want her and not because you think you should. A woman is looking to see if you are a man to the core but remember to always calibrate: if a woman says, "No," then she means "No." Masculinity doesn't react to emotions from the feminine and instead just reflects them back at her. This is a sign of a man strongly in touch with his core.

Feminism has created a lot of social conditioning and ended up repressing a lot of men. We start to think that women don't like men, that they don't want to be taken, or that a man should supplicate. What women are really saying, though, is that they want men to be present with them. They don't want men to feel superior or inferior; they just want to feel you. If you are distant and not connecting to her, then she will get very angry. Watching television, playing on the computer, doing sports, masturbating—these are all activities of man, they all give us that feeling of freedom. But, as a man, take responsibility for making sure your life is in balance. Your woman will appreciate just one hour of quality time with you rather than six hours of distracted time.

Remove notions that love is a card with a heart on it, or a trip to Paris, or a bunch of flowers. These gestures might demonstrate that you've made an effort and invested into the relationship, but they aren't love. Everything around us that is living is love—you just need to allow yourself to connect to that feeling. Get in touch with your core and love will well up inside of you. A woman's deep heart, often ignored, wants to be touched. You can do this by feeling her deep heart through love.

Chapter 15:
Going Out With Friends

Sometimes you might go out to meet people by yourself. I think this is great. Meeting people by yourself builds character and self-esteem. The most important thing to remember when you are on your own is to start talking to people as quickly as possible. Procrastination is your worst enemy. Less thinking, more talking.

The rest of the time you'll find yourself going out with other people—people who are in and know about the PUA Method community, also known as PUA Method Planet, and people that aren't.

When out with people who are in the community you are able to take more social risks. What do I mean by this? Well, the great thing about this community is that it gives you the opportunity to have as many social interactions with women over a two-year period as the average man will have in his entire life.

When you are out with people who know about this community—wingmen, as we call them—try new things. Push the interactions as far as they will go, test new theories and material. Don't say something is ineffective until you've tested it twenty times. Just like going to the gym, you increase your stamina each time you go out. This will expand your comfort zone and difficult things will start to feel easy.

WINGMAN RULES

You and your wingman should be friends. Make sure you and your wing have commonalities other than women. Find out what similar interests you have—music, sports, hobbies—and hang out together outside of game. Having cool friends in your life will raise your survival value dramatically when demonstrated in front of women.

When talking to women, big each other up rather than putting each other down. By putting your friends down you are sub-communicating to women that you have low-value friends. People tend to hang out with other people with a similar value to their own. Ever dated a hot woman? You will notice that all her friends look very similar to the woman you are dating; almost clones. A woman's value is based primarily on sexual replication, your value is based primarily on survival. If she presumes you have low-value friends, then she will also think that you are low-value too for being with them. Always be proud of your friends.

Never fight over a woman. There's a simple rule: whoever approaches first can choose the woman he wants. There should be no excuses or deviations from this rule. Use secret phrases to let your wing know who your target is. For example, you could say, "Watch out for this one—she's trouble," to let your wing know this woman is your target.

If you're with your wing, make sure you escalate in sync. If this doesn't happen, it is often one of the main ways a wing can wreck a good interaction. If you and your wing are talking to two women and one woman is a lot more giggly than the other, then the less giggly one will drag the other woman away. She will recognize that the happier woman is going to have sex and, because she isn't in that state of mind herself she'll end the interaction. If both women are in a similar state of arousal, then this won't happen.

Isolate in a cool way. You don't want your wing to pick up his woman and carry her out of the venue. Your woman will immediately begin to freak out and look to see what is happening. This usually spells the end of the interaction as the other woman's comfort levels have been exceeded. It's not the woman who was picked up that has lost comfort but her friend. When in a group interaction bear in mind everyone's comfort levels, as they can influence the outcome.

It is usually best to escalate physically and verbally in isolation away from the group. This simple step removes the necessity of having to deal with the friends' comfort levels and makes your wing's job a lot easier.

If you are much more experienced than your wing, then it is often good to let him go first and get the added bonus of being confident and spontaneous in the approach. You can then enter the conversation, talk to the other woman, and isolate her away from your wing as quickly as possible. That way both women won't end up talking to you and you can develop a connection with just one of them.

If your wing has really bad approach anxiety, then don't try to push him to approach. Just treat it as a solo night and bring him in when you need him and hang out with him after interactions. He will get bored soon enough and start to approach for himself.

If your wing enters your conversation and you don't want him there, then tell him you'll catch up with him in a bit. Then tell the woman that he's some guy from work.

If a guy enters your conversation and you don't know him or don't really care, then ignore him and keep talking to the women. If he tries to engage you, then say, "That's cool, man," and continue talking to the women. He will get bored, walk off, and your value will be raised.

A lot of these wingman rules take practice to develop. Until you find a good wing, it is usually good practice just to go out with guys and open for yourself. When the set is over, you have a social base to go back to.

Take responsibility for yourself to have a good night. If your wing is not approaching, then take it upon yourself to do so.

SOCIAL CIRCLE RULES

When out with non-PUA Method Planet friends or women, then you need to use a lot more social calibration. The general rule is that you are sociable with everyone.

Speak mainly with your friends. If you're on the way to the bar or the restroom and you see a woman that you want to talk to, then that is fine. When your friends ask what you said, then you play it down rather than bragging. Raising your value too high will make your friends feel bad about themselves and like they do not want to hang out with you again. You can say that you were asking what's good to drink or just had a bit of small talk.

Never try to teach your non-community friends how to approach on a night out, unless they ask you to. Don't encourage them to talk to women with you. Let your friends join you if they want to, and, if they ask for help, then you can give them advice.

When out with women you will find that you get approached so you don't need to do much. Qualify the women approaching you almost straightaway. If you are out with women your value will be high and so it will seem like you are trying too hard if you use any attraction material. Let other women see you when you are out with your female friends, then strike up a conversation with them later in the evening.

Don't push social boundaries as much when out with friends. Instead just be sociable, build connections, and have fun. The more memories and history you can build with your friends, the stronger that emotional bond will become. If you forget to build rapport, then those friends won't stay friends for very long. It will feel like you are just using them to meet women.

CALIBRATE, BUT DON'T PLAY GAMES IN A RELATIONSHIP

A woman can tell when a guy is playing games with her emotions. When she senses this she will often play her own games. This can lead to jealousy issues and lots of problems. Instead, calibrate. There should be a continuous process of punishment and reward in your relationships. This is not dog training. This is actively demonstrating your boundaries and values. If someone does something that you don't like, then pay them less attention. If a positive behavior is shown, then reward the person with attention.

If a woman tries to make you jealous, then don't retaliate; instead just tell her that you like / love her and there is no need to play games. Then ignore this behavior in the future and reward her positive behavior more. If she is lacking your attention, then give it to her for positive reasons.

If the woman continues to exhibit bad behavior, then make it very clear that this is unacceptable. If it continues, be willing to walk away. Most people don't change, especially if they aren't into self-help. So, if your new girlfriend is going out and getting drunk a lot of the time, it is probably best not to get into a serious relationship.

Obviously, as people get older their priorities change and a lot of hot women get fed up with the attention they get at nightclubs. However, there are also a lot of hot women that have never liked clubbing and prefer to do things at home. Life is abundant, so you can be selective about who you choose to have around.

FINAL THOUGHTS

Finally, as I leave you now, I want to wish you an abundance of peace and love for your life. I know we've never met face-to-face, but it sure feels like we have, doesn't it? I feel very grateful to have been able to share parts of my life and my skills with you and I hope that I have moved you in some special way. I hope that you will stay in touch wtih me, write to me, enrol on a PUA Method Bootcamp, join me on our residential course, or that we just have the chance to cross paths. I look forward to meeting you and hearing about your dating and life successes. Until then, remember: be real, be authentic, and live a life of love and passion. Spread the word and help bring more positive light into this world. It is down to you now.

Peace and love,

Robert King (Kingy)

INDEX

Acknowledgments

My Mum, Dad, Brother, Russell Brand, Bruce Lee, Eckhart Tolle, Steve Pavlina, The Dalai Lama, Timothy Ferris, Eban Pagan, Neil Strauss, Mystery, Tyler, Cupid, Jordan, Cieran, Max, Paul Janka, Hypnotica, Beckster, Badboy, Ross Jefferies, Wayne Elise, David X, Asian Playboy, Johnny Wolf, Og Furious, Sebastian, Steve Jabba, Deeboy, Skeletor, Adrian, Catnap, Phoenix, Majik Craze, Gecko, Monika, Roberto, Peter N, Adam P, Luke, Alan P, Harley Johnstone, Dan Mcdonald.

Further Reading and Online Resources

Zen Mind, Beginner's Mind, Shunryu Suzuki (Shambhala Publications, 2011)

Tao of Jeet Kune Do, Bruce Lee (Ohara Publications, 1975)

The Three Pillars of Zen, Philip Kapleau (Bantam, 1996)

A New Earth, Eckhart Tolle (Penguin, 2009)

The Power of Now, Eckhart Tolle (Hodder, 2001)

Awaken The Giant Within, Anthony Robbins (Pocket Books, 2001)

How to See Yourself As You Really Are, The Dalai Lama (Rider, 2008)

An Open Heart, The Dalai Lama (Mobius, 2002)

Mastery, George Leonard (Penguin 1992)

The Game, Neil Strauss (Canongate, 2007)

Driven from Within, Michael Jordan (Atria Books, 2006)

Striking Thoughts: Wisdom for Daily Living, Bruce Lee (Tuttle Publishing, 2002)

Think and Grow Rich, Napoleon Hill (Capstone, 2009)

The Secret, Rhonda Byrne (Simon & Schuster, 2006)

The Optimum Nutrition Cookbook, Patrick Holford and Judy Ridgway (Piatkus, 2010)

www.realsocialdynamics.com

www.venusianarts.com

www.tonyrobbins.com

Contact

For official live pick-up training with zen and lifestyle design with the author Robert King (Kingy) and instructors, visit www.puamethod.com or email kingy@puamethod.com